ALL YOU NEED TO KNOW

&

A GUIDE TO OTHER SELF HELP ALTERNATIVES

VOLUME 1

EUNICE FINNEY
AND
BARBARA BRADSHAW

E & B PUBLICATIONS

First published in 1993 in Great Britain by
E & B Publications
PO Box 322, Stafford, ST16 2PA
Tel No 0785 228866
Reprinted April 1994

Cover and Art Work by Geoffrey Barker

Photographs by Peter Rogers (Photographic) Ltd.

Typeset by E & B Publications

Printed by Panda Press (Stone) Ltd.

I.S.B.N. 1-897697-00-7

**This book is dedicated to our husbands,
Mike and Bill,
for their help and encouragement
during our endless hours of writing.**

Contents

Acknowledgements

Our grateful thanks to Jane Landick, Moyra McLaughlin and Annette Christie who have typed the manuscript. Without their help it would have been impossible to achieve the finished result. Their patience during constant changes and alterations at the proofing stage was greatly appreciated. Also thanks are extended to Mike Tiernan for his help in proof reading.

We will be forever grateful for the artistic abilities of Geoff Barker, without which our book would look very plain and ordinary, our sincere thanks.

Martin Watt and Clive Bendon, to whom we must extend our gratitude and thanks for their help with the information and data on Essential Oils. Their knowledge, expertise and patience has been greatly appreciated.

As our knowledge of computers is somewhat limited we would like to extend our thanks to Bill Klotz who has spent many hours sorting out those very irritating technical problems.

To Barry Tunnicliffe our thanks, for his technical knowledge and expertise in the printing industry. For his encouragement and patience when we have been unable to meet some of our deadlines.

Finally but by no means least our appreciation and thanks must go to our family and friends who have supported and encouraged us throughout and acted as honorary babysitters on numerous occasions.

Introduction

Aromatherapy - All You Need to Know is the first volume of three books. A common interest in Aromatherapy inspired the idea for this book and the other two volumes - Aromatherapy for Pregnancy and Birth and Aromatherapy for all the Family.

We strongly recommend that you read the first chapter in its entirety especially if you are using essential oils for the first time. We make no apology for some repetition in all the books, this is inevitable when cross referencing some items.

This book is aimed at the individual who has no professional training in the field of Aromatherapy but would like to know more. It is designed in an easy to read format with user friendly symbols.

Over the years through personal experience and using essential oils for our own families we have become aware of the excellent healing properties which these plant extracts have. We hope you enjoy reading this book and share the experience and benefits of Aromatherapy, its pleasant aromas and therapeutic effects.

Barbara. Eunice

Barbara Bradshaw Eunice Finney

Chapter 1

Essential Oils -
The Dos and Don'ts

All you need to know about essential oils and how to use them. This chapter is full of useful information and facts. Essential reading for all.

Chapter 1

Essential Oils -
The Dos and Don'ts

The use of aromatic plants has been around for many thousands of years. Prehistoric man is known to have used plant remedies. The Egyptians used aromatic oils three thousand years before Christ, for embalming purposes.

A French chemist called René Gatefosse in the 1930s worked in a laboratory blending perfumes. Whilst at work one day, he burnt his hand and plunged it immediately into the nearest bowl of liquid, which happened to be the essential oil of **Lavender**. It was then that he realised the wonderful healing and antiseptic properties of **Lavender** essential oil and he was amazed that the burn did not blister or scar. It was Gatefosse who first used the term 'Aromatherapy' as it encapsulated the idea of a pleasant aroma with therapeutic properties.

During the 1950s, Dr Jean Valnet, a French doctor, who worked with the wounded during the Second World War, did most of the modern research into essential oils. Many French doctors still today prescribe essential oils to be taken orally for medical conditions and the practice of Aromatherapy is recognised by the pharmaceutical industry. You cannot buy essential oils over a shop counter in France as they are prescribed drugs only. At about the same time, Madame Marguérite Maury, who was a biochemist and also French, concentrated on using oils externally for massage.

- Aromatherapy has increased in popularity over the past few years especially with more emphasis being placed on a healthier lifestyle.

- Members of the Royal Family are reported to use essential oils and Margaret Thatcher is said to have found them helpful in relieving stress while residing at Number 10 Downing Street.

- Aromatherapy is recognised as a purely holistic treatment.

What are Essential Oils?

- Essential oils are made by extracting oil from flowers, roots, leaves, bark, wood, spices and herbs. The liquid is not really an oil, but perhaps is better described as an essence.

- Essential oils are obtained by using the following methods of extraction - Enfleurage, Absolute, Distillation, Expression and Solvent Extraction.

Enfleurage This is an ancient method for extracting essences from delicate plants such as Jasmin and Rose. Glass sheets are coated with purified fat. The freshly picked petals are strewn onto the fat and fresh petals are replaced every day for up to about 8 weeks. When the fat has completely absorbed the essence, the pomade, as it is called, is diluted with alcohol and vigorously agitated. The alcohol is allowed to evaporate to separate the essential oil. This method is rarely used today.

Absolute This is a prepared fragrance material. A solvent such as de-natured alcohol is used to dissolve the fragrance materials out of the concrete. Nowadays, this process is done in carefully controlled equipment under partial vacuum and in factories. To ensure full extraction from the concrete the process is often repeated several times and so different grades of absolute can be produced. The first extraction is the best grade as it will contain more of the volatile 'top notes' required by the perfumery trade. The absolute can be further processed usually by solvent extraction (as described previously) to yield the pure essential oil.

Distillation This is also an ancient technique for the extraction of essential oils. It has been known since at least the 10th century. Distillation is the usual method of extracting oil from hardier aromatic plant material. The plant material is placed in a still. Hot water or steam is passed through it and the essences are given up to the steam which then passes through a cooling process to be condensed and collected in vats where the oil and the watery distillate can be separated.

Expression The majority of the citrus fruit essential oils are obtained from this ancient and simple form of extraction. The peel of the fruit is simply pressed. Various machine methods are used these days, because hand expression is very labour intensive and therefore expensive. Most expressed oils are then distilled before they are sold. This process 'cleans up' the oil, removing undesirable plant constituents.

Solvent Extraction This method produces the most concentrated and most expensive oils. The plant material is placed in a receptacle to which is added a solvent - petroleum, acetone, ether or carbon dioxide. This is then heated slowly. The resulting mixture is then filtered, agitated with alcohol and distilled. It is used to preserve the sensitive top notes which are very volatile chemicals destroyed by hot distillation.

How do Essential Oils Work?

- Aromatherapy works to influence the physical, emotional and spiritual wellbeing.

- Most essential oils have antiseptic and anti-bacterial properties and some oils are anti-viral.

- The smell of essential oils can be inhaled via the olfactory system which sends messages to the brain. Aromatic particles can also pass through the nasal passage to the lungs.

- Essential oils are usually categorised as stimulating, relaxing, uplifting and calming.

How to Purchase your Essential Oils?

- Always purchase from a reputable company to ensure that your essential oils have not been adulterated. The words 'pure' and 'natural' may not always mean what the names suggest.

- Some essential oil suppliers are members of EOTA - Essential Oils Trade Association. The members of this Association guarantee pure and unadulterated essential oils. This is the EOTA symbol: EOTA

- Essential oils can be purchased from health shops, some beauty shops, mail order and usually from your own Aromatherapist.

- If the essential oils on sale are all the same price it is a sign that the oils could be synthetic or adulterated. However, premixtures are often sold at the same price, so be sure what is being offered, before you purchase.

- Rose, Jasmin, Melissa organic and Neroli are the most expensive essential oils to purchase and are usually only available in a shop on request.

- Only purchase essential oils which are in dark glass bottles.

- There are approximately 20 drops of essential oil in every 1ml and 200 drops in a 10ml bottle.

Storing Essential Oils

- Keep the bottle tops of all essential oils tightly closed as they can evaporate quickly if left exposed to the air.

- All essential oils should be kept in dark coloured bottles away from light and heat. They can be stored in a refrigerator.

- Essential oils will keep on average for about two years. However, the citrus oils are not as effective and only have a shelf life of six months. **Sandalwood** and **Frankincense**, however, are said to mature with time.

- Once mixed, massage oils should be stored in a dark bottle, the properties will then remain effective for three to six months. You can purchase brown bottles and jars cheaply from a chemist.

- Never store essential oils in plastic containers - it does alter their properties considerably and as the oils are very strong it could cause the plastic to melt.

Carrier Oil or Creams

- A carrier oil or cream is used to dilute essential oils, so that they can be used directly on the skin.

- Carrier oils are also known as base oil or vegetable oil. Mineral oils, for example baby oil, are not suitable.

- The most popular carrier oil is Sweet Almond oil.

- Other carrier oils include Apricot Kernel, Fractionated Coconut, Corn oil, Grape oil, Hazelnut oil, Peanut oil, Safflower oil, Soya oil, Sunflower oil.

- Other **fixed** oils can be added to the base oil at a dilution of 10% for additional therapeutic properties. These are: Avocado Pear oil, Borage Seed oil, Carrot oil, Evening Primrose oil, Jojoba oil, Olive oil, Sesame Seed oil and Wheatgerm oil, Rosehip and Camellia.

- There are many sorts of carrier creams which are suitable, for example, unperfumed cream such as Vitamin E cream.

- Carrier oils can be purchased from health shops or chemists. Sweet Almond oil is used by various ethnic cultures and can often be obtained from Asian shops much more cheaply.

- When measuring carrier oil it is useful to know that one teaspoon is approximately 5ml and one dessert spoon is approximately 10ml.

Cautionary Notes

- **Never take essential oils internally unless prescribed by an aromatherapist or herbalist.**

- The vast majority of essential oils are perfectly safe for home use, providing they are used correctly.

- Many essential oils mentioned in this section are not freely available, however, the information is provided as a precautionary measure, should you encounter them being offered for sale.

- Never assume that an essential oil will have the same properties as credited to the whole plant from which it is extracted.

- As with any concentrated substance, you must keep essential oils **out of the reach of children** and never leave the bottle where a child can take off the top and consume the contents. Some essential oils are more harmful to children if accidentally swallowed, this caution will be represented by the symbol shown.

Children

- Never use neat **essential oils** on the skin with the exception of **Lavender** and **Tea Tree** in certain circumstances. If neat essential oil accidentally comes into contact with the skin, rub any suitable carrier oil or milk on to the affected area. This will dilute the essential oil.

- Do not use an essential oil as a food flavouring without expert guidance.

- The following oils are unsuitable for use at home: **Alan Root (Inula), Bitter Almond, Birch, Bergamot (expressed, F.C.F. is safe), Boldo, Cade, Calamus, Camphor (unrectified), Cassia, Cinnamon Bark, Colophony, Costus, Croton, Horseradish, Mustard, Opoponax, Peru Balsam, Rue, Sassafras, Savin, Tansy, Tolu, Terebinth, Turpentine (unrectified), Verbena, Wintergreen, Wormseed.**

- The following oils cannot legally be sold to the public: **Croton, Savin, Wormseed. Sassafras** is banned in food products in the United Kingdom.

- The following oils are very strong and require caution when being used. For example, if you use them in a bath, never use more than one or two drops. The same advice should be followed when using essential oils by other methods. These oils include: **Aniseed, Benzoin, Camphor (rectified), Clove, Eucalyptus, Ginger, Juniper, Black Pepper, Pimento, Peppermint, Sage, Savory, Spearmint, Thyme,** this caution will be represented by the symbol shown.

Drops Limited

- Oils which can cause irritation on sensitive/damaged skin, if you suffer from perfume/cosmetic sensitivity or any allergic skin condition include: **Aniseed, Benzoin, Camphor (rectified), Clove, Eucalyptus, Ginger, Juniper, Black Pepper, Pimento, Peppermint, Sage, Savory, Spearmint, Thyme,** this caution will be represented by the symbol shown.

Skin Irritation

- These oils if used undiluted or to excess may cause severe irritation and damage to delicate skin tissues: **Birch, Camphor, Cassia, Cinnamon Bark, Cinnamon Leaf, Clove, Eucalyptus, Ginger, Juniper, Peppermint, Pimento, Rosemary, Sage, Savory, Spearmint, Tansy, Thyme, Turpentine,** this caution will be represented by the symbol shown.

Skin Irritation

- Some oils listed below may only cause irritation in some people with sensitive skin: **Bay, Cardamon, Citronella, Clary Sage, Fennel, Hyacinth, Jasmin, Juniper, Lemon, Litsea Cubeba, Lovage, Mimosa, Orange, Pine, Rose, Spearmint, Tolu, Ylang Ylang.**

- Essential oils which must not be used prior to sunbed treatment or exposure to strong sunlight include: **Angelica root, Bergamot expressed, Caraway, Cassia, Cedarwood, Cinnamon Bark, Cumin, Ginger, Grapefruit, Lime expressed, Mandarin, Orange expressed, Patchouli, Rue, Verbena,** this caution will be represented by the symbol shown.

Sun and Sunbed

- People who experience skin problems following the use of cosmetic products, the consumption of spicy or highly flavoured foods, need to be careful in their choice of essential oils. If a particular essential oil causes your skin to come out in a rash or makes it hot and itchy, then do not use that oil again, or try using it at much lower dilutions to see if you can find a level your skin can tolerate. There are numerous other different essential oils you can try which should not cause similar problems. For instance, if you react to **Lavender** then you could try **Sandalwood** as an alternative as it is unrelated chemically.

- The following essential oils should not be used generally on moles, extensive areas of freckles, sunburnt skin, senile patches, melanoma, pre-melanoma or other skin cancers: **Citrus Fruit Oils, Calamus, Sassafras, Turpentine.**

- All concentrated products including essential oils are best avoided during the first few months of pregnancy. After the third or fourth month, there are many oils which can be used in Aromatherapy treatments and some which are particularly effective for relaxation. For further information see Volume 2.

- Essential oils which should not be used during pregnancy include: **Basil, Clove, Cinnamon, Mugwort, Hyssop, Fennel, Juniper, Marjoram, Myrrh, Origanum, Pennyroyal, Sage, Savory, Tansy, Thyme, Tarragon, Thuja, Wintergreen**, this caution will be represented by the symbol shown.

Pregnancy

- If you suffer from epilepsy, do take care when using strong, stimulating essential oils such as **Fennel, Hyssop, Sage, Wormwood or Rosemary.**

- If essential oils are **splashed into the eyes,** immediately flush with water, if irritation continues flush with cold milk. If this treatment does not alleviate the stinging or irritation, seek medical assistance.

- Essential oils on the finger tips should be removed by gently scrubbing with a strong solution of washing up liquid. You must not rub the eyes, if you have essential oils on your fingers, as severe eye irritation can be caused by: **Cinnamon, Peppermint etc**.

- If neat essential oils are not removed from the fingers, they can easily be transferred to other delicate parts of the body and cause stinging and inflammation. If this occurs, wash the affected area well with warm soapy water, dry thoroughly and, if necessary, apply handcream, medicated cream or, if nothing else is available, a small amount of butter, margarine or vegetable cooking oil.

- Some essential oils are flammable therefore avoid any naked flame.

- Take care that neat essential oils do not come in contact with polished surfaces as they may cause damage.

- Accidental excess consumption of essential oils - if this occurs, you must seek immediate medical assistance. If a person shows signs of illness after consuming a few drops of oil, this is probably a very rare allergic reaction similar to a bee sting allergy and immediate medical treatment should be sought. When you visit the hospital, always take with you the essential oil which has been consumed.

Essential Oils for Babies and Children

- Essential oils should only be used in small quantities for babies and children.

0 - 2 years	**One drop** of essential oil diluted in 10ml Almond oil or milk. The only essential oils suitable for use are **Lavender** or **Roman Chamomile.**
2 - 5 years	**One to three drops**. Essential oils most suitable for use are **Lavender, Mandarin, Rose** or **Roman Chamomile.** Most essential oils are perfectly safe to use at this age and are preferable to some drugs.
5 - 12 years	Use as directed for adults but halve the number of drops of essential oil.
12 years onwards	Use as directed for adults.

- The most suitable methods of use for babies and children are: bath, massage, compress, room vaporiser, on the edge of the pillow, nightwear, radiator, ointment, light bulb ring and room spray.

How to use Essential Oils

- Essential oils are often sold without clear instructions on the bottle stating how to use them.

The number of drops of essential oils suggested under each method is the quantity recommended for adults. To use essential oils for babies and children, use the recommended drops as stated in the previous section.

Bath

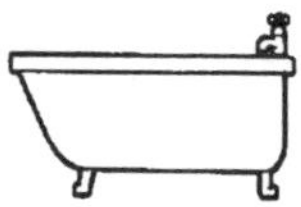

1. Run a bath of warm water.
2. Add **six drops** of essential oil.
3. With your hand, agitate the bath water so that the essential oil is fully dispersed.
4. Relax in the bath for 10-15 minutes only.

- Do not get the water too hot as the essential oil will evaporate quickly.
- Close the bathroom door so that you can take full advantage of the aromatic vapours which you will inhale.
- If you have dry skin add **six drops** of essential oil to 5ml (a teaspoonful) of carrier oil or milk, mix and then add to your bath.
- Whilst you are relaxing in the bath, if you are able to, turn over onto your tummy, this will ensure maximum benefits from the essential oils.

Shower

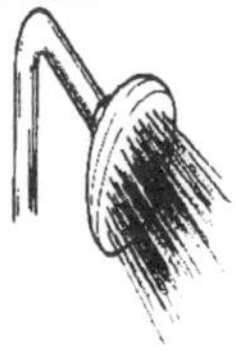

1. Enjoy a warm shower in the usual way.
2. Mix **six drops** of essential oil in 10ml of milk or unfragranced shower gel .
3 Apply onto a sponge and rub all over the body, remaining under the water spray at all times

- The shower is not as relaxing as a bath when using essential oils, but can be quite stimulating and ideal at the start of the day.
- The warming vapours can be inhaled with maximum benefit.

Compress

1. Fill a bowl with water.
2. Add **four to five drops** of essential oil.
3. Place a small piece of cotton material (i.e. small handtowel, muslin nappy, face flannel or handkerchief) in the bowl.
4. Wring out excess water and place on affected area.

- As a general rule, **hot** compresses are for chronic conditions and should be removed when they become cold.

- As a general rule **cold** compresses are for acute conditions and should be renewed when blood heat is reached.

- Alternate **hot** and **cold** compresses aid the healing process in conditions where massage cannot be used.

Bidet

1. Fill with warm water.
2. Add **three drops** of essential oil.
3. Mix the essential oil and water thoroughly.

- The vaginal area is of course very sensitive so be sure there are no globules of essential oil left on the surface of the water in the bidet.

- If you are not fortunate enough to have a bidet, a portable one can be purchased at a reasonable cost.

Portable Bidet

1. Place portable bidet on top of the toilet pan and then lower the toilet seat.
2. Fill bidet with warm water.
3. Add **two drops** of essential oil.
4. Mix the water and oil thoroughly so there are no globules of essential oils left on the surface of the water.

- When you have finished using the bidet, tip the water into the toilet. Do not flush until the next person uses the toilet as the water and any remaining essential oil will act as a very good disinfectant for the toilet itself.

- An easy way to fill your portable bidet is to use a shower attachment on the wash basin or bath taps and place the nozzle directly over the bidet.

- Your portable bidet will enable you to take your own personal hygiene kit wherever you go.

- Portable bidets are available at a very reasonable price.

Jug Douche

1. Boil a kettle and allow the water to cool or use cold bottled water.
2. Measure out one litre of water in a jug and mix thoroughly with **six drops** of essential oil.
3. Lift both the lid and seat of the toilet.
4. Sit well over the toilet pan, pouring the solution over the vulval area.
5. Gently dry the area using a soft towel kept for this purpose.

- If your kettle has any limescale, take care not to get this into the douche.

- You can use a bottle to carry out this treatment but take care when using plastic bottles - the water may come out faster than anticipated.

Sitz Bath

1. Run a few inches of warm water into a bath or a bowl.
2. Add **three drops** of essential oil and agitate the water.
3. Sit in the bath for a few minutes.

- Sitz baths are also known as hip baths and are particularly useful after childbirth.

- You could also use a baby's bath or a large washing up bowl, purchased especially for this use.

Footbath

1. Prepare a washing up bowl or foot spa with warm water.
2. Add **four drops** of essential oil and agitate.
3. Soak your feet for 15-20 minutes.

- This method is useful if you do not have time for a bath. The soles of your feet are covered with reflex points and the essential oils act on these areas.

Massage

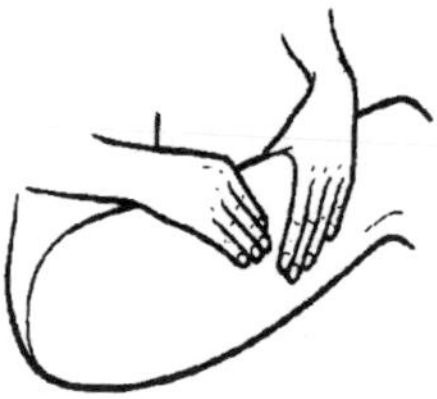

1. Prepare your massage oil i.e. 10ml of carrier oil with **five drops** of essential oil.
2. Mix the carrier oil and essential oil well.
3. The essential oils are transferred to the body via the carrier oil.

- Massage is very skilled and we do suggest that you consult a trained therapist.

- Massage is the most popular method of application used by trained therapists.

- For preparation of carrier oils for massage, use the following proportions for the formula:

  i.e. 50ml of carrier oil plus 25 drops of essential oil.
  or
  30ml of carrier oil plus 15 drops of essential oil.

- For a quick and simple calculation, it is useful to note that by dividing the total number of mls of carrier oil by two (2), it will equal the number of required drops of essential oil (e.g. $10 \div 2 = 5$). Therefore 5 drops of essential oil would be added to 10ml of carrier oil.

- Massage should not be carried out if any of the following conditions are present: bruising or easily irritated skin, heart condition, circulation problems especially varicose veins or thrombosis, infectious skin conditions such as eczema or psoriasis, open wounds, scars from recent surgery, recent fractures, inflamed painful joints, abdomen during pregnancy and menstruation and diabetes as the skin may be very delicate.

- Self massage using essential oils at home is ideal when you have a few aches and pains.

- Ensure the room where the massage is to be carried out is comfortably warm.

Water Bowl

1. Pour hot water into a bowl.
2. Add **eight to ten** drops of essential oil.
3. Place bowl on a firm and sturdy surface and the aroma will fill the room.

- Take care if you have small children around. Do not leave the bottle of essential oil in a child's room.

Inhalation from Bottle

1. Remove the top from the essential oil bottle.
2. Take a sniff and inhale.

- Children must be supervised if this method is used.

Inhalation on Tissue

1. Place **one drop** of essential oil on the tissue.
2. Inhale directly from tissue.

- You can put the tissue with essential oils down your bra or in a shirt pocket and continue to sniff the aroma throughout the day.

- Do not use the method above if you are a breast feeding mother.

Pillow and Nightwear

1. Place **one drop** of essential oil on the edge of a pillow and/or on nightwear.
2. You will inhale the essential oil as you sleep and it should help you to breathe more easily.

- This method is particularly useful if you have a cold or suffer from insomnia.

- A few essential oils display a strong colour which could mark linen. These include: **Rose, Jasmin, Mandarin, German Chamomile, Patchouli and Vetiver**. You may choose to use these essential oils by putting one drop on a piece of cotton wool and placing it inside the pillow case.

Ointments

1. Fill a 30ml brown screw-topped jar with carrier cream or lotion.
2. Add **fifteen drops** of essential oil.
3. Stir and mix well.

- Carrier cream and brown screw-top jars can easily be obtained from the local chemist.

Light Bulb Ring

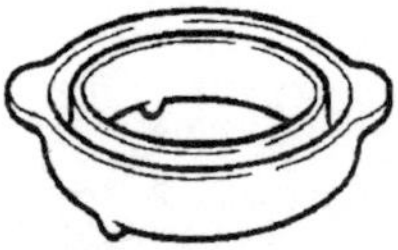

1. Add **two to three drops** of essential oil to the light bulb ring.
2. Place light bulb attachment on top of the electric light bulb.
3. Turn on the light.

- **Beware** - some essential oils are flammable so do not get any oil on the light bulb itself.

Vaporiser

1. Fill a vaporiser three quarters full of water and stand it on a firm and sturdy surface.
2. Add between **three and six drops** of essential oils.
3. Light the candle.

- The candle in the vaporiser will heat the water which then gives off the vapour into the room.

- Never leave your vaporiser on when you go out of the house.
- Always keep the water topped up in your vaporiser.
- A vaporiser may also be known as a diffuser.
- Electric vaporisers have become much more popular and of course, safer. We would recommend only electric vaporisers for use in hospitals as naked flames are hazardous where oxygen and anaesthetic gases are in use.

Radiator

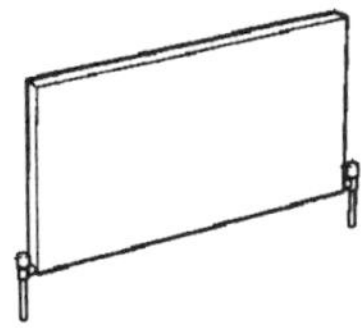

1. Soak a cotton handkerchief or cotton wool ball in water.
2. Add **four to six drops** of essential oil and place on the radiator.

- The heat from the radiator will dry out the handkerchief and evaporate the essential oil vapours into the room.
- This method is safe and ideal for the nursery. Essential oils such as **Peppermint, Thyme, Eucalyptus** will sting a baby's eyes if the vapours become concentrated so you must ensure there is a reasonable air flow in the room.
- Beware, some essential oils may cause a slight staining on the paint surface of radiators.

Room Spray

1. Add 300ml of water to a plant spray.
2. Add **eight to ten drops** of essential oils and vigorously shake well, before each use.
3. Spray as required in room on carpets, curtains etc. Do not get the spray on polished surfaces.

- It is always a good idea to purchase a new plant spray especially for this purpose.

Steam Inhalation

1. Pour hot (not boiling) water into a bowl.
2. Add **two to three drops** of essential oil.
3. Lean over the bowl, covering your head with a towel. Keep eyes closed while inhaling.
4. Take deep breaths through your nose and stay under the towel for approximately 5 minutes.

- Take care with the hot water, especially if small children are around.
- Ideal treatment for sniffly colds and runny noses.
- Electric inhalers can now be purchased.

Car

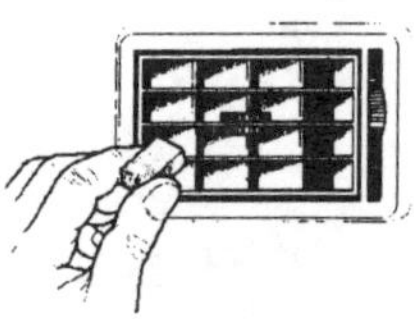

1. Purchase a new foam sponge and cut into small pieces.
2. Dampen the sponge piece with water.
3. Add **four drops** of essential oil.
4. Place between the heater vents in the front of your car and turn on the heater.
5. The foam squares do not last long so throw away after the second or third time of use.

- One sponge will cut up into approximately 100 small pieces.
- Keep some spare foam squares, premixed blends and water in a spray bottle in the glove compartment of your car. You may then change the aromas to fit your mood.
- This method of use is ideal if you are on a long journey, feel tired and need stimulation.
- Also useful if you have agitated children in the car, however, ensure that the calming essential oils used do not send the driver to sleep.

Essential oils can be applied to the body by water, carrier, or used as an inhalation.

Useful Information

- Should you think your skin may be sensitive to essential oils then do a patch test. This is easily done by measuring 5ml of carrier oil and adding 2 drops of the suspect essential oil. Then rub a small amount of the formula onto your forearm. If a reaction occurs you will know you are sensitive to the essential oil which has been tested. To relieve irritation caused by a sensitive reaction, rub some Sweet Almond oil or cold milk on the affected area.

- If you wish to consult a trained aromatherapist and do not know of a local practitioner, contact the International Society of Professional Aromatherapists or the International Federation of Aromatherapists. Their addresses are listed in Appendix 2. They will provide you with an up to date list of trained aromatherapists in your area. See Volume 1, Chapter 6.

- If you wish to pre-blend essential oils yourself, use bottles which have previously contained essential oils, but firstly wash the bottle, cap and top thoroughly, in soapy water and then sterilise in a Milton Steriliser or baby's steam steriliser. Do not sterilise at the same time as other feeding equipment. Once the bottles have been sterilised, rinse off any Milton solution. Vinegar cleans the metal plate at the base of steam sterilisers and will get rid of any odours left behind by the essential oils. So do not throw away your old essential oil bottles as they could be useful.

- When using essential oils always try to ensure that you use more than one, as this enhances the therapeutic effect on the body.

- Do not use the same essential oil every day because after a month or so you will become immune to it and it will not have the desired effect.

- Always smell your essential oils - if the smell is at all offensive to you, do not use that oil as it is unlikely it will have any beneficial effect for you. Remember your nose and sense of smell is telling your body what is right for you. Some trained aromatherapists do rely heavily on their patients' sense of smell and before carrying out a massage they will ask the patient to smell the oils which the therapist proposes to use. If any oils are disliked, they would be omitted from the massage blend.

- Aromatherapists and textbooks can give contradictory information. This does confuse beginners. You will find in some books that totally differing essential oils are suggested to treat the same medical condition. Every aromatherapist has his or her preference for certain oils and this does influence the choice made when deciding which oils to use for a particular case. Also, the School of Aromatherapy which the aromatherapist has trained at, will influence the formulae used in his or her future practice, to some degree.

- Some essential oils are thicker than others, for example Sandalwood, Chamomile, Rose absolute, Jasmin absolute and Vetiver. These oils take longer to come through the dropper. You can warm the bottle in the palm of your hand or hold it over a warm radiator, the heat will help the oil to flow quicker.

- Do not be tempted to use a few extra drops of essential oil thinking that it will have a better therapeutic effect. In fact it is well known that less essential oils sometimes has a more potent effect.

Chapter 2

Essential Oils Profiles

The properties of essential oils are studied in detail in this chapter which has been ideally arranged for easy reading and reference purposes by Martin Watt, the author of the Plant Aromatics Reference Manual.

Chapter 2

Essential Oils Profiles

Essential oils from plants vary in the same manner as good wine. The composition varies depending on soil type, geographical location, weather conditions, time of harvesting, variety of plants used and on processing methods. Most oils are supplied to the perfumery and food trades who require reasonably standardised raw materials. For this reason the oils are frequently blended from a number of different growing regions, as are most table wines, and this blending often improves the overall character of the oil. There are limited volumes of oil available direct from local growers and these, like vineyard wines, possess their own distinct characteristics.

The actual percentages of the different natural chemicals which make up the oils are not given as they can vary tremendously depending on the origin of the oil. The **odour** character of an essential oil is often dependent on tiny traces of the plant's chemicals and is not necessarily due to the major components found in the oil. The major components often contribute to known medicinal effects such as with Menthol from Peppermint, Linalol in Lavender, etc.

Most of the properties attributed to the oils in this book are those recognised for **external** application, and only a few are for consumption, such as Peppermint, Aniseed and other flavouring oils. It is not recommended you consume oils without expert advice, as some aromatherapy oils have synthetic fragrance chemicals added which may not have the same action as a natural oil. Likewise, oils sold as aromtherapy blends should not be consumed.

When referring to antiseptic or anti-bacterial essential oils it should be remembered that the constituents of the oils vary with age and the properties cannot always be relied upon.

Aniseed

(Illicium verum - star anise tree)
(Pimpinella anisum (true aniseed)

Main countries of origin: Star-anise - China. Pimpinella - East Europe, India, Turkey and other countries.

Source of oil: Star-anise - dried whole fruits. Pimpinella - the seed.

Major constituents: Trans-Anethole.

Properties: Stomach calming, expectorant.

Uses: Widely used at low levels for food flavouring and in medicines under professional guidance only. Not very often used for massage.

Cautionary notes: There are reports of irritation caused to people with sensitive skin. The World Health Organisation is currently reviewing the maximum levels allowed in foods due to concerns about the effects of excess consumption.

Extra caution: This oil differs from most essential oils in that it tastes very pleasant. It is therefore VITAL to keep it away from children. A small bottle consumed would result in illness and a large (25ml) bottle could be lethal to a young child.

Basil

(Ocimum basilicum, Ocimum gratissimum and numerous other varieties)

Main countries of origin: Worldwide.

Source of oil: Flowers, leaves and stem.

Major constituents: Vary enormously, depending on the variety, but Methyl Chavicol, Linalol and Methyl Cinnamate dominate certain varieties.

Properties: Anti-depressant, envigorating.

Uses: Anxiety, depressive states, catarrh, appetite stimulant; high Linalol varieties tend to be relaxing rather than stimulating.

Cautionary notes: This oil should not be used for home cooking as, depending on the variety of plants used, it may contain a natural chemical which could cause health problems if consumed in excess. There is no evidence that this chemical causes any problems when the oil is used in Aromatherapy massage, baths or in room fragrances.

Extra caution: Dangerous if swallowed by a child.

Bay

(West Indian Bay)
(Pimenta racemosa)

Main countries of origin: West Indies.

Source of oil: Leaves.

Major constituents: Eugenol, Chavicol and Myrcene.

Properties: Fragrance.

Uses: Used mainly in the perfumery and cosmetics trades. Not used much in Aromatherapy massage.

Cautionary notes: Keep away from children. This Bay oil is totally different from the European Bay Leaf used in cooking and this oil should **not** be used for food flavouring.

Bergamot

(Citrus aurantium var. bergamia)

Main countries of origin: Mediterranean countries, Africa, Americas.

Source of oil: Fruit peel.

Major constituents: Limonene, Linalyl acetate, Linalol, Monoterpenes.

Properties: Anti-depressive, refreshing, relaxing.

Uses: Emotional instability, anxiety, loss of appetite, oily skin and acne.

Cautionary notes: Unmodified expressed Bergamot oil applied to the skin, even when well diluted, can produce a condition known as photosensitization. This results in skin damage occurring following exposure to sunlight or sunbeds.

The only Bergamot oil which is totally safe is marked F.C.F.; this means that the bergaptenes and other naturally occurring chemicals which can lead to skin damage have been reduced to safe levels.

Black Pepper

(Piper Nigrum)

Main countries of origin: Indonesia, Malaysia, India, Comoro Islands.

Source of oil: The fruit.

Major Constituents: Mono-terpenes.

Properties: Aromatic, stimulant, tissue warming.

Uses: An aid to digestion, muscular stiffness, joint pain, as an inhalant for coughs, colds, influenza. This oil is more suited to local application rather than general body massage.

Cautionary Notes: This oil should never be used neat on the skin as it can cause blistering. People with sensitive skin should ensure it is well diluted to avoid skin irritation and/or burning sensations.

Cajuput

(Melaleuca leucadendron)

Main countries of origin: Indonesia, Malaysia, Phillipines, Vietnam, Australia.

Source of oil: Leaves and twigs.

Major constituents: 1,8-Cineole, α-Terpineol.

Properties: Aromatic stimulant, tissue warming, antiseptic, expectorant.

Uses: Muscle stiffness, joint pain, headaches, as inhalant for colds and bronchitis, acne, psoriasis etc., toothache.

Cautionary notes: Keep away from children.

Camphor Oil

(Cinnamomum camphora and varieties, also other unrelated trees)

This oil should not be confused with the white crystalline form which is pure Camphor; the oil may in fact only contain low levels of Camphor.

Main countries of origin: China, Japan, Taiwan, Australia, Africa, Spain.

Source of oil: Chipped wood.

Major constituents: Depends on oil type. There are three main types with Camphor and Linalol, Camphor and Saffrole and Cineole-Terpineol-Camphor.

Properties: Tissue warming, reduces muscle pain, antiseptic, stimulant, insect repellent.

Uses: Primarily for muscular aches, joint pain and fibrositis, but also colds, influenza, bronchitis and any difficult breathing. This oil is only suited to local application rather than general body massage.

Cautionary note: This oil should never be used neat, or for more than a few days without a break. It is best left for professional use as there are several dangers associated with its use.

Cedarwood

*(**Texan** - Juniperus mexicana, **Virginian** - J. virginiana, Atlas - Cedrus atlantica, **Chinese** - J. procera, also other varieties are used around the world. True **Lebanon Cedar** oil is not available, due to the few trees left being a protected species)*

Main countries of origin: North America, Morocco, Algeria, China.

Source of oil: Chipped wood.

Major constituents: Dependent on variety, but common components are Cedrenes, Cedrol.

Properties: Insecticidal, soothing relaxant, anti-catarrhal.

Uses: Skin problems especially eczema and dermatitis, also acne and psoriasis, muscle stiffness, joint pain, bronchitis and any lung problems, urinary tract problems, mental exhaustion.

Cautionary notes: Not advisable neat on the skin. Do not confuse with cedar leaf which is entirely different and much more dangerous.

Chamomile German

(Matricaria recutita - also named Chamomilla recutita and Matricaria chamomilla)

Main countries of origin: Europe, Egypt, Americas, and many other countries.

Colour: Usually deep ink blue.

Source of oil: Flowers.

Major constituents: α-Bisabolol, Chamazulene, Bisabolol oxides.

Properties: Anti-bacterial, anti-inflammatory, anti-spasmodic.

Uses: Wounds, skin problems especially eczema and dermatitis, muscle stiffness, joint pain, bronchitis and any lung problems, nervous instability, hay fever and other allergies.

Cautionary notes: There are a few rare reports of skin irritation, particularly after long term use.

N.B. Can be spelt Camomile.

Chamomile Moroccan

(Ormenis mixta or Ormenis multicaulis)

Main countries of origin: Morocco.

Source of oil: Flowering tops.

Major constituents: Santolina alcohol, α-Pinene, Bisabolene.

Properties: Unverified.

Uses: Unverified.

Cautionary notes: The chemistry of this oil is substantially different from Roman or German Chamomile; unlike most essential oils it does not appear to have undergone scientific testing for skin irritation potential or toxicity. It may well possess useful therapeutic properties but there is little traditional evidence as to what it may safely be used for. The oil was originally produced for the perfumery trade. The price of this oil is substantially lower than GOOD QUALITY Roman or German Chamomile.

N.B. Can be spelt Camomile.

Chamomile Roman

(Chamaemelum nobile - also called Anthemis nobilis)

Main countries of origin: English is considered the best but it is also produced in the whole of Europe, South America and many other countries.

Source of oil: Flowers.

Colour and smell: This oil ranges from a transparent bluish green when new, but soon changes to a light green with a fruity smell.

Major constituents: Quite variable depending on the plant variety, but generally the Esters of Angelic, Butyric and Tiglic Acids.

Properties: Anti-bacterial, relaxant to sedative, anti-inflammatory.

Uses: Most types of wounds, skin disorders, insomnia, mental relaxation, tension headaches, inhalant for hay fever and nasal congestion, and for a wide range of other ailments.

Cautionary notes: There are a few rare reports of skin irritation particularly after long term use.

N.B. Can be spelt Camomile.

Clary Sage

(Salvia sclarea)

Main countries of origin: Russia and Eastern Europe, Morocco, America, China, France, Italy.

Source of oil: Flowering tops, or tops plus seed.

Major constituents: Sclareol, Linalyl acetate, Linalol.

Properties: Anti-depressant, soothing nerve relaxant, aphrodisiac for men and women.

Uses: Nervous exhaustion, anxiety, P.M.T., skin disorders, aphrodisiac for men and women.

Cautionary notes: The fragrance is powerful and can overwhelm some people.

Clove

(Eugenia caryophyllata)

Main countries of origin: Comoro Islands, Madagascar, Indonesia, Brazil.

Source of oil: Clove buds, leaves and twigs produce different grades of oil.

Major constituents: Eugenol.

Properties: Stimulant, anti-spasmodic, antiseptic, anodyne.

Uses: Food flavouring, stomach upsets, toothache and a wide range of medicinal uses under professional supervision only.

Cautionary notes: Not advisable for massage due to its skin irritating properties and the unreliable composition of the oil.

Cypress

(Cupressus sempervirens and other varieties, depending on origin)

Main countries of origin: France, Italy, Portugal, Spain, North Africa.

Source of oil: Needles, twigs and cones.

Major constituents: Varies but Monoterpenes dominate.

Properties: Relaxing and refreshing, anti-cough, anti-spasmodic, astringent.

Uses: Spasmodic coughs, influenza, excitability, oily skin and acne.

Cautionary notes: None.

Eucalyptus

(Eucalyptus globulus, E. radiata and hundreds of other varieties are used)

Main countries of origin: Worldwide production.

Source of oil: Leaves.

Major constituents: 1,8-Cineole and Monoterpenes.

Properties: Stimulant, anti-spasmodic, antiseptic, anodyne.

Uses: In medicinal agents for most respiratory tract ailments, as an inhalant for nasal congestion, as a rub and inhalant for chest infections, for local application to infected minor wounds, chicken pox and shingles, for muscular aches and joint pain, as an anti-microbial room spray.

Cautionary notes: Not advisable for full body massage, but ideal for local use or in a bath to clear the head.

Extra Caution: This oil is one of the most useful but this effectiveness also means it is one of the most dangerous if it is consumed. Deaths have occurred from as little as 5ml. It is therefore essential that it is kept away from children.

Fennel

(Foeniculum vulgare)

Main countries of origin: France, Italy, Greece, North Africa, India, Spain.

Source of oil: Seed.

Major constituents: Trans-Anethole.

Properties: Anti-nausea, anti-spasmodic, anti-fungal.

Uses: Spasmodic coughs, stomach upsets, colic, indigestion. The whole seed extract is used in gripe water.

Cautionary notes: Can cause skin sensitivity so not advisable for massage other than local use, well diluted and short term.

Frankincense

((Boswellia thurfera and other varieties)

Main countries of origin: Somalia, Ethiopia, Middle East, Western India.

Source of oil: Resin exuded after cuts are made in the tree bark; this resin is then distilled or CO2 extracted to obtain the oil.

Major constituents: Tremendously variable depending on variety, mainly Monoterpenes and Olibanol.

Properties: Astringent, antiseptic, anodyne, comforting.

Uses: Since ancient times Frankincense has been used for a wide variety of ailments, a principal ingredient in incense, used for damaged skin particularly ulcers, mental relaxation for 'unwinding', to ease difficult breathing such as asthma, coughs, colds.

Cautionary notes: None known.

N.B. The correct name for Frankincense is **Olibanum.**

Geranium

(Pelargonium graveolens, P. odorantissimum many other varieties and clones)

Main countries of origin: Egypt and North Africa, China, Reunion and many other countries.

Source of oil: Flowers and leaves.

Major constituents: Geraniol, Citronellol, Citronellyl formate, Menthone.

Properties: Relaxing, but mentally uplifting, skin ailments.

Uses: Nervous tension, P.M.T., highly recommended for the bath to 'unwind', oily skin, herpes, hormonal instability.

Cautionary notes: There are one or two reports of skin irritation being caused by this oil, but this is EXTREMELY rare.

Ginger

(Zingiber officinalis and other varieties)

Main countries of origin: China, West Indies, West Africa, India and others.

Source of oil: Rhizomes.

Major constituents: α and β-Zingiberene, ar. Curcumene, Farnesene.

Properties: Warming to the body, circulatory stimulant, anti-microbial.

Uses: Muscle and joint soreness and pain, nausea, colds and influenza, poor leg circulation.

Cautionary notes: This oil should not be used NEAT on the skin, some oils are stronger than others and some can cause inflammation and soreness. Keep away from the eyes.

Grapefruit

(Citrus paradisi)

Main countries of origin: Americas, Africa, Cyprus, Israel and others.

Source of oil: Fruit peel.

Major constituents: Limonene.

Properties: Stimulating, anti-depressant.

Uses: Circulation, digestive, cellulite, exhaustion, constipation.

Cautionary notes: Some oils may be mild photosensitizers so do not use before going into bright sunlight or before using sunbeds.

Ho Leaf

(Cinnamomum camphora, Linalol varieties)

Main countries of origin: China, Japan and the Far East.

Source of oil: Leaves and wood.

Major constituents: Linalol.

Properties: Relaxant, antiseptic, anti-depressant.

Uses: Nervous irritability, P.M.T., anxiety, dry skin and deodorant.

Cautionary notes: Keep away from children.

Rosewood or **Bois-de-Rose** oil from South America is very similar in chemical composition to Ho Wood oil. Rosewood trees are being cut down faster than they are planted, so this oil comes from an unsustainable source.

Ho oils are mainly produced from the leaves of cultivated plantation trees. The trees have a useful life of about 20 years and they are continually replanted.

N.B. Sometimes call Ho Wood.

Hyssop

(Hyssopus officinalis)

Main countries of origin: France, Italy, Eastern Europe.

Source of oil: Flowers and leaves.

Major constituents: Pinocamphone, Camphor, β-Pinene, 1,8-Cineole.

Properties: Antiseptic, anti-spasmodic, relaxant.

Uses: Coughs, bronchial infections and difficult breathing, bruising.

Cautionary notes: Keep away from children.

Jasmin

(Jasminum grandiflorum and other varieties)

Main countries of origin: Egypt and North Africa, France, India, China.

Source of oil: Flowers.

Major constituents: Benzyl acetate, Linalol.

Properties: Relaxant, anti-depressant, anti-spasmodic, aphrodisiac.

Uses: Nervous instability, depression, P.M.T., psoriasis, impotence (male and female).

Cautionary notes: Most Jasmin on general sale is in its cruder ABSOLUTE form; pure Jasmin oil is available but is very expensive. Either type of Jasmin can cause irritation in people with sensitive skin. If you know you are allergic to perfumes and cosmetics, only use Jasmin if well diluted.

N.B. Jasmin can sometimes be spelt Jasmine.

Juniper

(Juniperus communis)

Main countries of origin: France, Italy, Eastern Europe.

Source of oil: The berries (best quality); the twigs and wood (cheaper).

Major constituents: α-Pinene, Cadinene, Limonene, Borneol.

Properties: Warming to the skin, antiseptic, relaxant/sedative.

Uses: Insonmia, anxiety, general stress, muscular problems and any arthritic condition, bronchial ailments, acne and over active skin.

Cautionary notes: Can cause skin irritation in some people particularly if it is not diluted enough.

Lavender

(Lavandula vera, Lavandula officinalis and many varieties and clones)

Lavandin-Lavandula fragrans and clones. This oil is quite different from Lavender and it is much cheaper; the smell is usually more harsh and camphoraceous. It is often used to adulterate and extend true Lavender oil.

Main countries of origin: Bulgaria, Yugoslav states, Hungary, Russia, France, England, Italy, Spain, South America and several other countries.

Source of oil: Flowering tops.

Major constituents: Linalyl acetate, Linalol.

Properties: Relaxant, anti-depressant, anti-spasmodic, antiseptic, analgesic, anti-nausea.

Uses: There is little that this oil cannot be used for, but its prime use is for all forms of stress relief/relaxation including insomnia, headaches, P.M.T., post natal depression, ideal for minor burns and any form of damaged skin, boils, acne, catarrh, colds, sore throats etc.

Cautionary notes: A very safe oil, but a few reports of skin irritation caused by hypersensitivity or prolonged exposure to the concentrated oil.

Lemon

(Citrus Limonum)

Main countries of origin: Worldwide.

Source of oil: Fruit peel.

Major constituents: Limonene,β-Pinene,γ-Terpinene, Citral.

Properties: Refreshing, stimulating, astringent, antiseptic.

Uses: Lethargy, to disinfect and fragrance rooms, throat infections, as an astringent for over-active skins.

Cautionary notes: Unrectified EXPRESSED oil can cause photo-sensitivity following exposure to sunlight or sunbeds. DISTILLED lemon is much safer. People who get skin irritation from cosmetics or perfume should only use this oil well diluted.

Lemongrass

(Cymbopogon citratus, Cymbopogon flexuosus)

Main countries of origin: India, Africa, West Indies, South America.

Source of oil: Above ground parts of grass like leaves.

Major constituents: Myrcene, Citronellal, Citral.

Properties: Relaxant, anti-depressant, anti-spasmodic, analgesic, antiseptic, anti-nausea.

Uses: Relief of stress, insomnia, stomach ailments including nausea, respiratory problems including asthma, muscular aches and pains, pain caused by bruised damaged tissues.

Cautionary notes: There are a few reports of skin irritation caused by hypersensitivity or prolonged exposure to the concentrated oil.

Mandarin

(Citrus reticulata and varieties)

Main countries of origin: Mediterranean countries, Americas, Africa.

Source of oil: Fruit peel.

Major constituents: Limonene, γ-Terpinene.

Properties: Relaxant, tonic.

Uses: Anxiety, insomnia, stomach ailments.

Cautionary notes: Might cause skin irritation if used at high levels or over a long period of time.

TANGERINE is similar in its composition and properties.

Marjoram
(European wild)

(Origanum vulgare)

Main countries of origin: Russia, Bulgaria, Italy, Spain.

Source of oil: Flowering tops.

Major constituents: Sabinene, Ocimenes, Sesquiterpenes.

Properties: Stimulant, tissue warming, analgesic.

Uses: Muscular aches, pains and strains, toothache, headache, relieving nasal and sinus congestion.

Cautionary notes: Keep away from children.

Marjoram
(Spanish wild)

(Thymus Masticina and other similar thymes)

Main countries of origin: Mostly from Spain.

Source of oil: Flowering tops.

Major constituents: 1,8-Cineole, Linalol, Borneol.

Properties: Antiseptic.

Uses: Aches and pains, nasal congestion, headaches.

Cautionary notes: May cause skin irritation.

Marjoram
(Sweet)

(Origanum majorana also Marjorana hortensis)

Main countries of origin: Central and Eastern Europe, Egypt and North Africa, France, Turkey.

Source of oil: Flowering tops.

Major constituents: cis-Sabinene hydrate, γ-Terpinene, Terpinene-4-ol.

Properties: Anti-bacterial, tissue warming, analgesic, anti-spasmodic.

Uses: Muscular aches, pains and strains, relaxant, insomnia, anxiety, for relieving nasal and sinus congestion.

Cautionary notes: Keep away from children.

Melissa
(Lemon Balm)

(Melissa officinalis and several varieties)

Main countries of origin: France, Ireland, Italy.

Source of oil: Leaves.

Major constituents: Citronellal, Geranial, Neral.

Properties: Powerful relaxant, uplifting, antiseptic, anti-spasmodic.

Uses: For most types of stress relief, depression, anxiety, insomnia, ideal for P.M.T., may help reduce high blood pressure due to its relaxing property, stomach ailments of nervous origin, throat and chest infections.

Cautionary notes: May cause skin irritation, best used well diluted.

Melissa oil is very rare and due to this it is extremely expensive. Most 'Melissa' is either blends of oils with a similar aroma to Melissa such as Geranuim, Eucalyptus citriodora, Litsea, Lemon etc. or oils plus fragrance chemicals. The latter are best avoided for skin application as some of these fragrance chemicals can cause skin irritation. The blends of pure oils can be highly effective used in the bath for 'unwinding', for massage or just as room fragrance.

Myrrh

(Commiphora varieties)

Main countries of origin: East Africa, Ethiopia, Sudan.

Source of oil: Oleo-gum-resin exuded from the incised tree bark; this forms the Myrrh of commerce which is subsequently distilled or CO2 extracted to obtain the oil.

Major constituents: Monoterpenes, Sesquiterpenes.

Properties: Anti-inflammatory, anti-microbial, anti-spasmodic, healing.

Uses: For most skin ailments particularly leg ulcers, boils and damaged skin, throat and chest infections, gingivitis, mouth ulcers.

Cautionary notes: Must be kept away from children.

Myrtle

(Myrtus Communis)

Main countries of origin: Russia, Portugal, Italy, Morocco.

Source of oil: Flowers, leaves and twigs.

Major constituents: Very variable depending on source but Mytenyl acetate, 1,8-Cineole, Linalol, α-Pinene and Limonene.

Properties: Refreshing, stimulant, antiseptic, anodyne.

Uses: Muscular aches and pains, headache, relieving nasal and sinus congestion.

Cautionary notes: Although extracts of myrtle tree leaves and flowers in water have long been used for a wide variety of ailments, these properties will NOT all be present in the essential oil. There is little documentation of the use of the essential oil in medicine but the oil has been tested and is relatively safe.

Neroli
(Orange blossom)

(Citrus aurantium, subspecies amara)

Main countries of origin: Italy, France, North Africa and others.

Source of oil: Flowers of the bitter orange tree.

Major constituents: Linalol, Linalyl acetate, Limonene, β-Pinene.

Properties: Uplifting, anti-depressant, aphrodisiac, powerful perfume.

Uses: Stress relief, insomnia, nervous palpitations, to help normalise dry, sensitive skin, helps reduce high blood pressure if caused by stress.

Cautionary notes: Due to the expense of pure Neroli oil, there is a lot of oil around consisting partly or wholly of fragrance chemicals. This makes an acceptable perfume but is not advisable for massage.

Niaouli

(Melaleuca viridiflora and related species)

Main countries of origin: Indonesia, Australia, Tasmania, Madagascar.

Source of oil: Flowers, leaves and twigs.

Major constituents: Terpineol, 1,8-Cineol, Viridiflorol.

Properties: Anti-inflammatory, anti-microbial, healing.

Uses: Spots and boils, minor cuts and grazes, throat and chest infections.

Cautionary notes: Must be kept away from children.

Palmarosa

(Cymbopogon martini, variety motia)

Main countries of origin: India, Indonesia, Seychelles.

Source of oil: A type of grass.

Major constituents: Geraniol, Nerol.

Properties: Relaxant.

Uses: Skin infection, anorexia, fragrances.

Cautionary notes: None known.

Patchouli

(Pogostemon cablin)

Main countries of origin: Indonesia, Phillipines, Sumatra, Seychelles, Madagascan Islands, Brazil, Africa.

Source of oil: A type of grass.

Major constituents: Patchouli alcohol, Sesquiterpenes.

Properties: Stimulating and uplifting, sensual, anti-bacterial.

Uses: Depression, lethargy, dry or inflammed skin, acne.

Cautionary notes: If used at high concentrations, may cause mild skin photosensitivity.

Peppermint

(Mentha piperita, various cultivars)

Main countries of origin: Worldwide - the best is still grown in England.

Source of oil: Flowers and leaves.

Major constituents: Menthol, Menthones, Menthyl acetate.

Properties: Stomach calming, mental stimulant, cooling.

Uses: Universal food flavour, indigestion, flatulence, nausea, to waken up the mind if tired, headaches, to cool fresh bruises, well diluted to relieve itchy skin conditions like chickenpox.

Cautionary notes: This oil can cause great pain if it gets in the eyes so always handle carefully and wash hands well if it gets on the fingers. For use on the skin, it must be well diluted.

N.B. Cornmint *(Mentha Arvensis)* is widely sold as Peppermint.

Petitgrain

(Citrus aurantium sub sp. amara)

Main countries of origin: Most Mediterranean countries, Americas.

Source of oil: Leaves and twigs of the bitter orange tree.

Major constituents: Linalyl acetate.

Properties: Relaxing but mentally invigorating, deodorant.

Uses: Anxiety, lethargy, insomnia, tonic.

Cautionary notes: None.

Pine

(Often sold as Pinus sylvestris but worldwide hundreds of different pines are used to produce this oil)

Main countries of origin: Worldwide.

Source of oil: Needles and twigs.

Major constituents: α and β-Pinenes, Myrcene, Camphor, Camphene, Bornyl acetate.

Properties: Mental stimulant, refreshing, tissue warming, antiseptic.

Uses: Muscular and joint aches and pains, a few drops in a bath to start the day if you had a bad night, or ideal for muscular aches from gardening or similar strenuous work, as an inhalant or rub for chest infections, colds, coughs, sinusitis.

Cautionary notes: This oil may cause skin irritation if used at high levels or by those who are cosmetic sensitive.

Rose

(Rosa damascena and Rosa centifolia are the commonest varieties used for oil)

Main countries of origin: R. damascena - Bulgaria, Turkey, Morocco, India, former USSR states, China. R. centifolia - Morocco, Egypt, Tunisia, Yugoslav states, China. Small amounts of Rose oil is produced in other countries.

Source of oil: Flowers.

Grades: The ABSOLUTE is the most commonly available Rose extract; it is deep yellow to brown, thick and strongly aromatic. The Rose oil is obtained by distillation or solvent extraction; therefore Rose OIL is very much more expensive than the absolute.

Major constituents: Citronellol, Geraniol, Phenyl Ethyl Alcohol.

Properties: Anti-depressant, relaxant, anti-spasmodic, aphrodisiac.

Uses: Anxiety, P.M.T., insomnia, headaches, nervous palpitations, soothing and anti-inflammatory in skin care preparations.

Cautionary notes: The cruder absolute can cause skin irritation in sensitive people but as a pleasant aroma can be produced from very low dilutions, even cosmetic sensitive people may still benefit from this oil.

Rosemary

(Rosmarinus officinalis and other varieties and clones)

Main countries of origin: Worldwide.

Source of oil: Leaves and twigs.

Major constituents: 1,8-Cineole, Camphor, Monoterpenes.

Properties: Mental stimulant, refreshing, tissue warming, antiseptic.

Uses: Lethargy, to stimulate the mind, muscular and joint aches and pains, for headaches, sciatica, neuralgia, as an inhalant or rub for chest infections, colds, coughs, sinusitis.

Cautionary notes: None proven.

Sage
(Dalmatian)

(Salvia officinalis and clones)

Main countries of origin: Yugoslav states, Bulgaria, Turkey, Morocco, England, France, Italy and others.

Source of oil: Flowers, leaves and stems.

Major constituents: α-Thujone, 1,8-Cineole, Myrcene.

Properties: Tissue warming, anti-microbial, mental stimulant.

Uses: As an inhalant or diluted local application for bronchial infections, colds and influenza, sore throats, muscular aches and pains, mouth ulcers and gingivitis, nervous exhaustion.

Cautionary notes: Keep away from children.

Sage
(Spanish)

(Salvia lavandulaefolia and Salvia hispanorum)

Main countries of origin: Mainly Spain.

Source of oil: Leaves and flowering tops.

Major constituents: Camphor, Cineole, α and β-Pinene.

Properties: Tissue warming, powerful antiseptic, mental stimulant.

Uses: As an inhalant for bronchial infections, colds and influenza, as a massage oil for muscular aches and joint pain, sore throats and as a mild stimulant.

Cautionary notes: Should be well diluted or may irritate sensitive skin.

Sandalwood

(Santalum album)

Main countries of origin: India (Mysore), Sri Lanka, Indonesia.

Source of oil: Heartwood.

Major constituents: α and β-Santalol.

Properties: Anti-microbial, relaxant, anti-depressant.

Uses: Skin ailments, for throat and chest infections, as an 'unwinding' oil for stress related ailments.

Cautionary notes: Amyris oil, also known as West Indian Sandalwood is unrelated to the above but it is sometimes sold as 'Sandalwood'.

Spearmint

(Mentha spicata and other varieties and clones)

Main countries of origin: North America, Spain, Italy, Eastern Europe, China.

Source of oil: Flowering tops.

Major constituents: Carvone, Limonene.

Properties: Anti-spasmodic, stomach calming, mental stimulant.

Uses: Most types of stomach upsets including nausea, colic, to revive mental functions, similar uses to Peppermint.

Cautionary notes: Can irritate sensitive skin if not well diluted. Keep away from the eyes and children.

Tea Tree

(Melaleuca alternifolia)

Main countries of origin: Australia.

Source of oil: Leaves and twigs.

Major constituents: 1-Terpinen-4-ol, Monoterpenes.

Properties: Anti-fungal and anti-bacterial, reputed anti-viral.

Uses: Any infectious condition, athlete's foot, cuts, grazes, sores, cold sores, herpes, ulcers, insect bites, acne, boils, relieves irritable skin conditions, pruritis, haemorrhoids, minor burns, used in creams, lotions and pessaries for thrush, muscular pain.

Cautionary notes: If applied neat to the skin for spots, boils etc. may cause slight peeling of the dead layers of skin. Should only be used on areas of sensitive tissue such as for thrush if it is first well diluted. Poor grades of oil may only be very weakly antiseptic.

Thyme

(Thymus vulgaris and related species)

Main countries of origin: Spain, Morocco, Russia, China, Yugoslav states.

Source of oil: Flowers and leaves.

Grades: Two main types are available, known as red and white. Red should be orange to brown in colour and of a more herbaceous odour than the white oil which is redistilled red oil. In fact red oil is often simply a coloured version of white oil using paprika or similar colourants.

Major constituents: Thymol, Carvacrol, Borneol, α-Terpineol, Caryophylene, Camphene. Composition of Thymes is enormously variable depending on the variety used. If you do not know which you are buying, then for safety treat it as the most irritant type. Chemotypes are available such as Linalol type which will be less irritant but these will have different properties from normal Thyme.

Properties: Powerful anti-microbial, mental stimulant.

Uses: As an inhalant, or diluted local application for bronchial infections, colds and influenza, other uses in professional hands.

Cautionary notes: Thyme oils, depending on the type, can be very aggressive on the skin and must be greatly diluted before use. Ideally only use this way with professional guidance. Must be kept away from the eyes and children.

Verbena

(Lippia citridora and other species with similar fragrance)

Main countries of origin: France, North Africa, South America, China.

Source of oil: Flowering tops and leaves.

Major constituents: Enormously variable depending on variety.

Properties: A relaxing and refreshing room fragrance.

Uses: Should only be used for room fragrance.

Cautionary notes: This oil should NOT BE USED ON THE SKIN due to its powerful irritating property. Some varieties of Verbena may be suitable for use on the skin but unless the exact variety is known it is safer to avoid these oils. Keep away from children.

Vetiver

(Vetiveria zizanoides)

Main countries of origin: Dominica, Haiti, India, South America, Java, China.

Source of oil: A type of grass.

Major constituents: Vetiverol, Sesquiterpenes.

Properties: Mental relaxant, calming.

Uses: Palpitations due to stress or hyperactivity, anxiety, hyperventilation, room fragrance burners.

Cautionary notes: None.

Ylang Ylang

(Cananga odorata)

Main countries of origin: Comoro Islands near Madagascar; an oil called Cananga from the same variety of plants, is produced in Java and other countries, but this oil is not considered of the same quality as Ylang oil.

Source of oil: Large flowers from a tropical tree.

Major constituents: Linalol, Benzyl acetate, Sesquiterpenes, Geraniol.

Properties: Mental relaxant, calming, anti-depressant.

Uses: Stress reduction, hyperventilation, depression, anxiety, hyper-activity, may lower a high blood pressure if due to stress, room fragrance and sensual personal fragrance.

Cautionary notes: None.

Extra information: Ylang oil is produced in different grades which depend on the length of distillation. The most fragrant is EXTRA, then there is FIRST, SECOND and THIRD, all these have their uses but you will pay much more for EXTRA which is needed for high quality perfumes. There is another grade commonly available called Ylang complete which is usually a mixture of grades and produces a pleasant, reasonably priced aroma.

Listed below is a summary of the uses and properties pertaining to the relevant essential oils. Further uses are described within Volume 3, Chapter 2, A-Z of Family Use.

Acne: Bergamot, Cajuput, Cedarwood, Cypress, Juniper, Patchouli, Tea Tree.
Allergies: Chamomile German.
Analgesic: Lavender, Lemongrass, Marjoram (European), Marjoram (Sweet).
Anorexia: Palmarosa.
Anti-Bacterial: Chamomile German, Chamomile Roman, Marjoram (Sweet), Patchouli, Tea Tree.
Anti-Catarrhal: Basil, Cedarwood.
Anti-Depressant: Basil, Bergamot, Clary Sage, Grapefruit, Ho Leaf, Jasmin, Lavender, Lemongrass, Neroli, Rose, Sandalwood.
Anti-Inflammatory: Chamomile German, Chamomile Roman, Myrrh, Niaouli, Rose.
Anti-Fungal: Fennel, Tea Tree.
Anti-Microbial: Eucalyptus, Ginger, Myrrh, Niaouli, Sage (Dalmatian), Sandalwood, Thyme.
Antiseptic: Cajuput, Camphor Oil, Clove, Eucalyptus, Frankincense, Ho Leaf, Hyssop, Juniper, Lavender, Lemon, Lemongrass, Marjoram, Melissa, Myrtle, Pine, Rosemary.
Anti-Spasmodic: Chamomile German, Clove, Cypress, Eucalyptus, Fennel, Hyssop, Jasmin, Lavender, Lemongrass, Melissa, Myrrh, Rose, Spearmint.
Anti-Viral: Tea Tree.
Anxiety: Basil, Bergamot, Clary Sage, Ho Leaf, Juniper, Mandarin, Marjoram (Sweet), Melissa, Petitgrain, Rose, Vetiver.
Appetite Stimulant: Basil, Bergamot.
Aphrodisiac: Clary Sage, Jasmin, Neroli, Rose.
Arthritis: Juniper.
Asthma: Frankincense, Lemongrass.
Astringent: Cypress, Frankincense, Lemon.
Athlete's Foot: Tea Tree.
Boils: Myrrh, Niaouli, Tea Tree.
Breathing Difficulties: Hyssop.
Bronchial Infections: Hyssop, Juniper, Sage, Thyme.
Bronchitis: Cajuput, Camphor Oil, Cedarwood, Chamomile German.
Bruising: Hyssop.
Burns (Minor): Lavender, Tea Tree.

Cellulite: Grapefruit.
Chest Infections: Eucalyptus, Melissa, Myrrh, Niaouli, Pine, Rosemary, Sandalwood.
Chickenpox: Eucalyptus, Peppermint.
Circulatory Stimulant: Ginger, Grapefruit.
Colds: Black Pepper, Camphor Oil, Frankincense, Ginger, Pine, Rosemary, Sage, Thyme.
Cold Sores: Tea Tree.
Colic: Fennel, Spearmint.
Comforting: Frankincense.
Constipation: Grapefruit.
Cooling: Peppermint.
Coughs: Black Pepper, Cajuput, Cypress, Fennel, Frankincense, Hyssop, Pine, Rosemary.
Cuts and Grazes: Niaouli, Tea Tree.
Deodorant: Ho Leaf, Petitgrain.
Depression: Basil, Jasmin, Melissa, Patchouli.
Dermatitis: Cedarwood, Chamomile German.
Digestion: Black Pepper, Grapefruit.
Disinfectant: Lemon.
Eczema: Cedarwood, Chamomile German.
Emotional Instability: Bergamot.
Invigorating: Basil.
Excitability: Cypress.
Exhaustion: Grapefruit.
Expectorant: Aniseed, Cajuput.
Flatulence: Peppermint.
Gingivitis: Myrrh, Sage.
Haemorrhoids: Tea Tree.
Hay Fever: Chamomile German, Chamomile Roman.
Headaches: Cajuput, Marjoram, Myrtle, Peppermint, Rose, Rosemary.
Headaches - Tension: Chamomile Roman.
Herpes: Geranium, Tea Tree.
High Blood Pressure: Melissa, Neroli, Lavender.
Hormonal Instability: Geranium.
Hyperactivity: Vetiver.
Hyperventilation: Vetiver.
Indigestion: Fennel, Peppermint.

Influenza: Black Pepper, Camphor Oil, Cypress, Ginger, Sage, Thyme.
Inhalant: Eucalyptus.
Insect Bites: Tea Tree, Lavender.
Insect Repellent: Camphor Oil, Cedarwood.
Insomnia: Chamomile Roman, Juniper, Lemongrass, Mandarin, Marjoram (Sweet), Melissa, Neroli, Petitgrain, Rose.
Joint Pain: Black Pepper, Cajuput, Camphor Oil, Cedarwood, Chamomile German, Eucalyptus, Ginger, Pine, Rosemary.
Leg Circulation: Ginger.
Leg Ulcers: Myrrh.
Lethargy: Lemon, Patchouli, Petitgrain, Rosemary.
Lung Problems: Cedarwood, Chamomile German.
Menopausal: Clary Sage, Fennel, Geranium, Neroli, Rose, Ylang Ylang.
Mentally Uplifting: Geranium, Peppermint.
Mental Exhaustion: Cedarwood.
Mental Relaxation: Chamomile Roman, Frankincense, Vetiver.
Mental Stimulation: Petitgrain, Pine, Rosemary, Sage, Spearmint, Thyme.
Mouth Ulcers: Myrrh, Sage.
Muscle Aches and Pains: Camphor Oil, Eucalyptus, Ginger, Lemongrass, Marjoram (European), Marjoram (Sweet), Myrtle, Pine, Rosemary, Sage, Tea Tree.
Muscle Stiffness: Black Pepper, Cajuput, Cedarwood, Chamomile German.
Muscular Problems: Juniper, Marjoram.
Nasal Congestion: Chamomile Roman, Eucalyptus, Marjoram, Marjoram (Sweet), Myrtle.
Nausea: Fennel, Ginger, Lavender, Lemongrass, Peppermint, Spearmint.
Nerves: Clary Sage, Chamomile German.
Nervous Exhaustion: Clary Sage, Sage.
Nervous Instability: Jasmin.
Nervous Irritability: Ho Leaf.
Nervous Tension: Geranium.
Neuralgia: Rosemary.
Palpitations: Neroli, Rose, Vetiver.
P.M.T.: Clary Sage, Geranium, Ho Leaf, Jasmin, Melissa, Rose.
Pruritus: Tea Tree.
Psoriasis: Cajuput, Cedarwood.
Refreshing: Bergamot, Cypress, Lemon, Myrtle, Pine, Rosemary, Verbena.

Relaxing: Basil, Bergamot, Cedarwood, Chamomile Roman, Cypress, Geranium, Ho Leaf, Hyssop, Jasmin, Juniper, Lavender, Lemongrass, Mandarin, Marjoram (Sweet), Melissa, Palmarosa, Petitgrain, Rose, Sandalwood, Verbena.
Respiratory Tract: Eucalyptus, Lemongrass.
Sciatica: Rosemary.
Sedative: Chamomile Roman, Juniper.
Sensual: Patchouli.
Shingles: Eucalyptus.
Sinusitis: Marjoram (European), Marjoram (Sweet), Myrtle, Pine Rosemary.
Skin Disorders: Chamomile Roman, Clary Sage, Geranium, Myrrh, Palmarosa, Patchouli, Sandalwood, Tea Tree.
Skin - Dry: Ho Leaf, Neroli, Patchouli.
Skin - Itchy: Peppermint.
Skin - Oily: Bergamot, Cypress, Geranium.
Skin - Over Active: Juniper, Lemon.
Skin Warming: Ginger, Juniper.
Sores: Tea Tree.
Spots: Niaouli.
Stimulant: Black Pepper, Cajuput, Camphor Oil, Clove, Eucalyptus, Grapefruit, Lemon, Marjoram (European), Myrtle, Patchouli, Sage.
Stomach Ailments: Lemongrass, Mandarin, Melissa.
Stomach Calming: Aniseed, Peppermint, Spearmint.
Stomach Upset: Clove, Fennel, Spearmint.
Stress: Juniper, Lemongrass, Melissa, Neroli, Sandalwood, Vetiver.
Throat Infections: Lemon, Melissa, Myrrh, Niaouli, Sage, Sandalwood.
Thrush: Tea Tree.
Tissue Damage: Lemongrass.
Tissue Warming: Black Pepper, Cajuput, Camphor Oil, Marjoram (European), Marjoram (Sweet), Pine, Rosemary, Sage.
Tonic: Mandarin, Petitgrain.
Toothache: Cajuput, Clove, Marjoram (European).
Ulcers: Frankincense, Tea Tree.
Uplifting: Melissa, Neroli, Patchouli.
Urinary Tract: Cedarwood.
Wounds: Chamomile German, Chamomile Roman, Eucalyptus.

Chapter 3

Top, Middle & Base Notes

In this chapter the lasting quality of the fragrance is described by using the Top, Middle and Base Notes.

Chapter 3

Top, Middle & Base Notes

Essential oils can be categorised by their top, middle and base notes, which give an indication of the value of their fragrance.

Top Note - the fragrance will last for approximately 6 to 12 hours.
Middle Note - the fragrance will last for approximately 24 hours.
Base Note - the fragrance will last for approximately 2 days.

The notes are mostly used in the perfumery trade but some Aromatherapists also refer to them. The information is useful when essential oils are being blended by selecting one or two oils from each category. Once blended, the notes will of course be altered.

Listed below are some of the most popular essential oils under the appropriate notes.

TOP NOTES

Basil, Bergamot, Eucalyptus, Fennel, Ginger, Grapefruit, Ho Leaf, Lavender, Lemon, Lemongrass, Mandarin, Neroli, Petitgrain, Peppermint, Pine, Sage, Tea Tree.

MIDDLE NOTES

Chamomile, Cedarwood, Clary Sage, Frankincense, Geranium, Hyssop, Jasmin, Juniper, Lavender, Lemongrass, Marjoram, Melissa, Peppermint, Rose, Rosemary, Ylang Ylang.

BASE NOTES

Black Pepper, Cypress, Myrrh, Patchouli, Sandalwood, Vetiver.

A Few Blend Suggestions For Room Fresheners

Suggested methods of use:

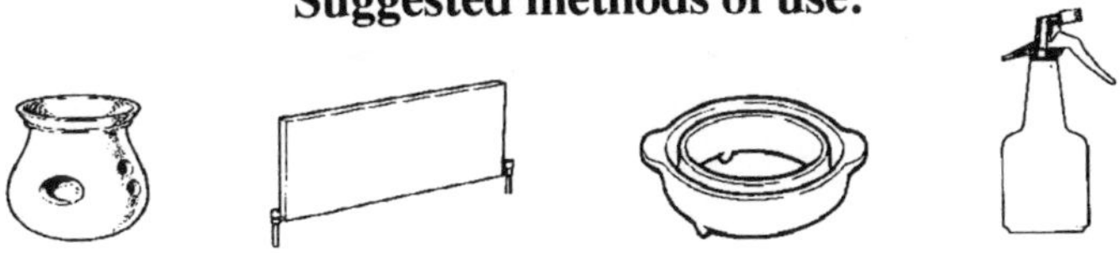

Antiseptic: Bergamot-3 drops, Lavender-2 drops, Tea Tree-1 drop

Refreshing: Lemon-3 drops, Grapefruit-2 drops, Lemongrass-1 drop

Relaxing: Bergamot-3 drops, Sandalwood-2 drops, Geranium-1 drop

or

Lavender-3 drops, Mandarin-2 drops, Ylang Ylang-1 drop

Special: Sandalwood-3 drops, Clary Sage-2 drops, Patchouli-1 drop, Rose-1 drop (optional)

N.B. All blends suggested use a combination of six drops of essential oils. When choosing the method of use check in Chapter 1 for the number of required drops of essential oils and adjust the blends accordingly.

Personal Blends

Chapter 4

Blending Properties

Essential oils blend together in endless combinations to provide varied and pleasant aromas.

Chapter 4

Blending Properties

The aromas which can be created when blending essential oils together are numerous. Although there are many combinations, some suggestions using the more popular essential oils, which blend well together, are listed below:

Basil
Bergamot, Black Pepper, Clove, Frankincense, Geranium, Grapefruit, Ho Leaf, Juniper, Hyssop, Jasmin, Lavender, Marjoram, Melissa, Neroli, Rosemary, Sage, Thyme

Bergamot
Basil, Cedarwood, Chamomile, Clary Sage, Clove, Cypress, Geranium, Ginger, Grapefruit, Ho Leaf, Jasmin, Juniper, Lavender, Lemon, Mandarin, Marjoram, Neroli, Pine, Rose, Rosemary, Sage, Sandalwood, Thyme, Ylang Ylang

Black Pepper
Basil, Clove, Fennel, Frankincense, Peppermint, Sandalwood

Cedarwood
Bergamot, Clary Sage, Cypress, Frankincense, Jasmin, Juniper, Lavender, Lemon, Neroli, Pine, Rose, Rosemary, Vetiver

Chamomile
Bergamot, Geranium, Lavender, Lemon, Marjoram, Melissa, Neroli, Patchouli, Rose, Vetiver, Ylang Ylang

Clary Sage
Bergamot, Cedarwood, Cypress, Frankincense, Geranium, Hyssop, Jasmin, Juniper, Lavender, Rose, Sandalwood, Petitgrain

Clove
Basil, Bergamot, Ginger, Lemon, Mandarin, Peppermint, Tea Tree, Thyme

Cypress
Bergamot, Cedarwood, Clary Sage, Juniper, Lavender, Lemon, Mandarin, Neroli, Marjoram, Pine, Rose, Sandalwood

Eucalyptus
Hyssop, Juniper, Lavender, Lemon, Lemongrass, Melissa, Pine, Rose, Rosemary

Fennel
Black Pepper, Geranium, Lavender, Lemon, Rose, Sandalwood

Frankincense
Basil, Black Pepper, Cedarwood, Clary Sage, Geranium, Ginger, Jasmin, Juniper, Lavender, Lemon, Lemongrass, Marjoram, Myrrh, Neroli, Patchouli, Rose, Rosemary, Thyme

Geranium
Basil, Bergamot, Chamomile, Clary Sage, Frankincense, Fennel, Ho Leaf, Jasmin, Juniper, Lavender, Lemon, Lemongrass, Melissa, Rose, Tea Tree, Thyme

Ginger
Bergamot, Clove, Frankincense, Lemon, Lemongrass, Mandarin, Patchouli, Sandalwood, Thyme, Vetiver

Grapefruit
Basil, Bergamot, Juniper, Lemon, Lemongrass

Ho Leaf
Basil, Bergamot, Geranium, Neroli, Rose, Sandalwood

Hyssop
Bergamot, Clary Sage, Eucalyptus, Lavender, Lemon, Mandarin, Rosemary, Sage

Jasmin
Basil, Bergamot, Cedarwood, Clary Sage, Frankincense, Geranium, Lavender, Lemon, Lemongrass, Neroli, Rose, Sandalwood, Ylang Ylang

Juniper
Basil, Bergamot, Cedarwood, Clary Sage, Cypress, Eucalyptus, Frankincense, Geranium, Grapefruit, Lavender, Mandarin, Patchouli, Rosemary, Sandalwood

Lavender
Basil, Bergamot, Cedarwood, Chamomile, Clary Sage, Cypress, Eucalyptus, Fennel, Frankincense, Geranium, Hyssop, Jasmin, Juniper, Lemongrass, Mandarin, Marjoram, Melissa, Myrrh, Neroli, Patchouli, Peppermint, Pine, Rose, Rosemary, Tea Tree

Lemon
Cedarwood, Chamomile, Clove, Eucalyptus, Fennel, Frankincense, Geranium, Ginger, Grapefruit, Jasmin, Juniper, Lemongrass, Neroli, Peppermint, Rose, Rosemary, Sage, Thyme, Vetiver, Ylang Ylang

Lemongrass
Basil, Eucalyptus, Frankincense, Geranium, Ginger, Grapefruit, Jasmin, Lavender, Lemon, Vetiver

Mandarin
Bergamot, Clove, Cypress, Ginger, Hyssop, Lavender, Juniper, Neroli, Tea Tree, Thyme

Marjoram
Bergamot, Chamomile, Cypress, Frankincense, Juniper, Lavender, Rosemary, Sage, Thyme

Melissa
Chamomile, Geranium, Juniper, Lavender, Neroli, Ylang Ylang

Myrrh
Clove, Frankincense, Ginger, Lavender, Patchouli

Neroli
Bergamot, Cedarwood, Cypress, Frankincense, Ho Leaf, Jasmin, Lavender, Lemon, Mandarin, Melissa, Patchouli, Petitgrain, Rose, Sandalwood

Patchouli
Basil, Bergamot, Cedarwood, Chamomile, Clary Sage, Frankincense, Geranium, Ginger, Jasmin, Juniper, Lavender, Lemon, Mandarin, Myrrh, Neroli, Petitgrain, Pine, Rose, Sandalwood, Thyme, Vetiver, Ylang Ylang

Peppermint
Black Pepper, Cedarwood, Clove, Ginger, Lavender, Melissa, Marjoram, Sage

Petitgrain
Bergamot, Clary Sage, Lemon, Neroli, Rose, Rosemary, Ylang Ylang

Pine
Bergamot, Cedarwood, Clove, Cypress, Eucalyptus, Ginger, Jasmin, Lavender, Lemon, Neroli, Rosemary, Sage, Sandalwood

Rose
Cedarwood, Chamomile, Clary Sage, Cypress, Fennel, Frankincense, Geranium, Ho Leaf, Jasmin, Lavender, Lemon, Neroli, Patchouli, Sandalwood, Vetiver, Ylang Ylang

Rosemary
Basil, Bergamot, Cedarwood, Eucalyptus, Frankincense, Juniper, Hyssop, Lavender, Lemon, Marjoram, Peppermint, Petitgrain, Sage, Tea Tree, Thyme

Sage
Bergamot, Hyssop, Lavender, Lemon, Melissa, Peppermint, Rosemary, Sandalwood

Sandalwood
Bergamot, Black Pepper, Clary Sage, Cypress, Fennel, Frankincense, Ginger, Ho Leaf, Jasmin, Juniper, Lavender, Lemon, Myrrh, Neroli, Pine, Rose, Sage, Vetiver, Ylang Ylang

Tea Tree
Bergamot, Clove, Geranium, Ginger, Lavender, Lemon, Mandarin, Rosemary

Thyme
Bergamot, Clove, Frankincense, Geranium, Lavender, Lemon, Mandarin, Melissa, Patchouli, Rosemary

Vetiver
Chamomile, Cedarwood, Ginger, Lavender, Lemon, Lemongrass, Patchouli, Rose, Sandalwood, Ylang Ylang

Ylang Ylang
Bergamot, Chamomile, Jasmin, Lavender, Melissa, Patchouli, Petitgrain, Rose, Sandalwood, Vetiver

A Few Blend Suggestions

Suggested methods of use:

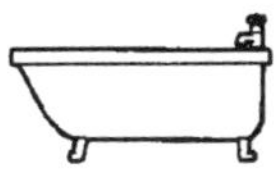
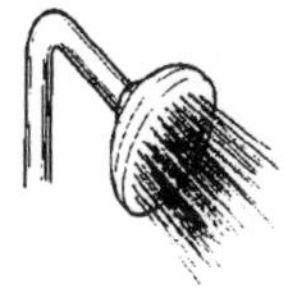
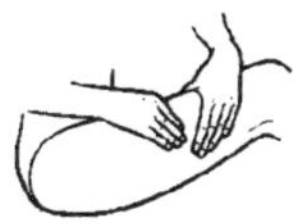

Relaxing: Lavender-3 drops, Marjoram (sweet)-3 drops

or

Lavender-3 drops, Geranium-3 drops

Stimulating: Rosemary-3 drops, Bergamot-3 drops

Refreshing: Lemon-5 drops, Peppermint-1 drop

Toning: Basil-3 drops, Grapefruit-3 drops

N.B. All blends suggested use a combination of six drops of essential oils. When choosing the method of use check in Chapter 1 for the number of required drops of essential oils and adjust the blends accordingly.

Personal Blends

Chapter 5

A Guide to the Cost of Essential Oils

A useful price reference which may help when you are planning your purchases of essential oils.

Chapter 5

A Guide to the Cost of Essential Oils

It is always advisable to purchase essential oils from a reputable dealer. If all the oils on sale are at the same price you can almost be sure that they are not pure essential oils. The price paid for essential oils may not indicate the quality and it is very difficult to prove the origin of organic essential oils, which are much more expensive.

We have prepared this guide to indicate the approximate price which you can be expected to pay. Most pure essential oils are imported and the price can alter from time to time. If a particular harvest has been poor and the country of origin has experienced extreme weather conditions this of course will affect the crops. The value of the "£" on the Money Market does fluctuate from time to time and this will affect the price of essential oils sometimes dramatically. Costs will also increase annually with inflation.

> This information is purely intended as an approximate guide for your reference and based on the average price of a **5 ml bottle** of pure essential oil, in **April, 1994**.

Under £3	Cajuput, Cedarwood, Eucalyptus, Lavender, Lemon, Lemongrass
Under £4	Aniseed, Camphor, Clove, Fennel, Grapefruit, Ho Leaf, Mandarin, Myrtle, Niaouli, Patchouli, Petitgrain, Pine, Rosemary, Sage, Tea Tree
Under £5	Basil, Bergamot, Black Pepper, Clary Sage, Cypress, Geranium, Ginger, Juniper, Marjoram, Palmarosa, Peppermint, Spearmint, Thyme, Vetiver, Ylang Ylang

Under £6	Chamomile (Maroc), Myrrh
Under £7	Frankincense, Sandalwood
Under £10	Chamomile (Roman)
Under £30	Melissa (organic)
Under £35	Chamomile (German/blue)
Under £50	Jasmin, Neroli, Rose

Personal Blends

Chapter 6

Choosing an Aromatherapist

In this chapter we discuss the importance of choosing a Professional Aromatherapist whom you can trust and feel relaxed with.

Chapter 6

Choosing an Aromatherapist

Choosing the right Professional Aromatherapist for you personally is very important and we have set out below a few general guidelines for your consideration:

- Write to the International Society for Professional Aromatherapists (ISPA) or the International Federation of Aromatherapists (IFA) and request an up to date list of practising therapists in your area; enclose a stamped addressed envelope for your reply.

- You may receive a recommendation for an Aromatherapist through a friend or advertisement. If that is the case, when contacting the therapist enquire about their training and any membership of a professional body ie ISPA or IFA.

- When you book your first appointment check how long your appointment will last. A detailed consultation and full body massage should take at least one hour.

- Your Aromatherapist is likely to ask you if you are taking any prescribed medication from your Doctor or any other herbal/homoeopathic preparation, if you are pregnant or suffering from any serious illness.

- It may be helpful to inform your GP that you are seeing an Aromatherapist but unless you are suffering from any medical condition it is not essential to inform your GP.

- If you have booked a full body massage you will be asked to undress to your bra/pants or underpants. You will then be asked to lie on a couch and be wrapped in towels.

- If you prefer to have only part of your body massaged, i.e. feet, hands, neck or shoulders this will take less time. A neck and shoulder massage is ideal if you are suffering from stress and will certainly help you unwind.

- Following the massage you may wish to relax for a few minutes before getting dressed. It is important that you drink plenty of water following your treatment as the therapist may have released toxins, which need to be flushed from the body.

- Do not have a bath or shower immediately after your massage. To get the maximum therapeutic benefit from the essential oils it is preferable to wait for at least 12 to 24 hours.

- You can expect to pay between £15 to £25 for a full body massage.

Personal Blends

Chapter 7

A to Z Guide to Self Help & Alternative Therapies

An A to Z of Complementary/Alternative Therapies which can be used alongside Aromatherapy.

Chapter 7

A to Z Guide to Self Help & Alternative Therapies

Many people are now turning to Complementary/Alternative Medicine and Natural self help treatment which can be carried out at home to aid relaxation and health.

In some areas the National Health Service is providing and referring patients to alternative/complementary practitioners. The Department of Health announced in December 1991 that Fundholding GPs may now directly employ complementary therapists within their practice staff. Non fundholding GPs may make referrals to such therapists but would need to seek the agreement of the purchaser of health care, which is usually the district health authority. It is the service purchaser who will pay for the treatment if permission is granted, although patients can ask their GP to refer them to a therapist.

The provider of the service (usually the GP) will have to demonstrate to the purchaser (usually the district health authority) that the treatment will be beneficial. The purchaser may also seek evidence of any clinical trials carried out on the therapy which has been requested. However, it is unlikely that such requests will be honoured because of the present financial climate which most health authorities find themselves in. Your GP may agree with complementary/ alternative therapies and be sympathetic to your request but he/she will unfortunately not have the final say if they are not a fundholding practice. If treatment is agreed with a therapist the GP will remain clinically accountable at all times.

If you require further information write to your MP or the Department of Health; the addresses are in Appendix ii. If you do not know the name of your MP the local library or Citizens' Advice Bureau will give you this information. At local level the Family Health Service Authority or your district health authority may be able to provide you with information. Their address and telephone number can be found in the local telephone directory or by contacting the Citizens' Advice Bureau.

Acupressure

Acupressure is a mixture of Acupuncture and Massage using the thumb and fingertips. Pressure is applied to pressure points which are believed to run through the 14 invisible channels known as meridians. This helps to ensure the balance of energy through the body.

Acupuncture

Acupuncture is an ancient Chinese therapy which involves the use of needles, which are inserted into the skin on points along the 14 meridians. This form of treatment is said to stimulate your own healing responses and balance the body.

Alexander Technique

The Alexander Technique when practised brings about an improvement in balance and co-ordination. The technique is normally passed on by a Teacher who will help you to improve your posture and balance and enable the pupil to use the body correctly by using the muscles effectively and releasing tension.

Auriculotherapy

Auriculotherapy is very similar to Acupuncture, involving the use of needles or modern electronic equipment on points of the outer ear. There are some 200 acupuncture points on the ear. The needles stimulate the energy points at the appropriate point relating to different parts of the body where healing is needed.

Bach Flower Remedies

Bach Flower Remedies are a natural, safe form of healing. There are 38 remedies which are made from an infusion of specific flowers in spring water which is preserved in alcohol. The remedies were developed by Dr Bach in the 1930s and are prescribed to fit a person's different mood, emotion or personality. Rescue Remedy, which is extremely popular, is a combination of 5 of the remedies and is used for emergencies when people are suffering from shock. Rescue Remedy is a 'MUST' for everyone's handbag. Bach Flower Remedies are readily available in Health Shops.

Chinese or Oriental Medicine

Chinese or Oriental Medicine is very different from conventional Western Medicine. It considers good health as a balanced and harmonious state of the vital life forces, i.e. the body's energy. Imbalances may be treated by using any of the Chinese medical principles comprising: Acupuncture; Herbal Medicine, when herbs are combined to formulate prescriptions; Chinese Massage, which is a combination of different massage techniques, and Chi King (Qi Gong), which is a gentle but powerful exercise programme to balance the body and mind, very similar to T'ai Chi.

Chiropractic

A Chiropractor is a therapist who specialises in diagnosing and treating disorders of the spine, joints and muscles. The treatment is carried out by skilful hand manipulation.

Colonic Hydrotherapy

Colonic Hydrotherapy or Colonic Irrigation as it is sometimes known is a cleansing of the bowel. It is carried out using a specialised machine by passing a tube into the rectum, then filtered water at a regulated temperature is guided through the colon, any deposits are siphoned away with the unclean water.

Colour Therapy

Colour Therapy is working to restore the body's impulses with the use of colour. The colour red, for example, is known to activate the circulation and stimulate energy. A therapist will use colour swatches to determine the correct colours for you.

Counselling

Counselling provides an individual with the opportunity to work through their feelings and conflicts with a counsellor on a one-to-one basis. Co-counselling is practised in pairs where both parties take on the role of counsellor and client for each other.

Crystals/Gem Stones

Crystals and gem stones are both formed of rock and minerals. The stones are said to help balance the body and promote good health and speed up the healing process. Each type of crystal is endowed with a specific energy.

Dowsing

Dowsing is the use of a pendulum or rods. It is generally understood that this works from radiation waves which can be detected. Once a question is asked the swing of the pendulum or rods identifies the answer. Many practitioners use this method to help diagnose and decide the appropriate treatment. It can also be used from a distance and some practitioners may request a sample of hair.

Dry Body Brushing

Dry Body Brushing is a self help technique used to stimulate the body and remove dead skin cells. It can be carried out at home using a natural bristle brush. With short firm upward strokes, starting with the soles and feet, legs, buttocks up to the arms, firm downward strokes for the shoulders, back and chest. Remembering always to work your brush towards the heart. For the stomach use a lighter stroke in a clock-wise circular movement. Brush your whole body except your face and avoid tender and sensitive areas. Always use a dry brush on a dry body and it is a good idea to take a bath or shower after the treatment. Body Brushing can be carried out while you wait for your bath to run. Brushes are available from any good Health Shop. To prevent over stimulation of the nervous system do not carry out this treatment after 6 pm in the evening. Avoid abdomen area when pregnant or when menstruating.

Floatation Therapy

Floatation Therapy promotes total relaxation and reduces stress. A floatation tank contains a shallow pool of warm water with a strong mineral and salt solution. The treatment lasts approximately an hour and is carried out in complete darkness.

Folk Remedies

Traditional Medicine is often known as 'Folk Remedies' or 'Country Cures' passed down through generations. Many suggested remedies use plants and herbs, however some suggestions are quite outrageous by today's standards.

Healing

Healing can be carried out in several forms. Absence or Distance Healing where the client may never meet the healer. The Laying on of Hands, Spiritual Healing or Faith Healing when the healer makes direct contact with the patient.

Herbal Medicine

Herbal Medicine treats the whole person by the use of individually prescribed plant remedies and natural diet. A Medical Herbalist will treat disease, prevent disease and carry out health promotion. It is probably one of the most ancient of all the healing arts.

Homoeopathy

Homoeopathy treats the cause of the illness rather than the symptoms. Homoeopaths believe that they must treat the whole person. The homoeopathic remedy given will usually imitate the patient's symptoms, treating like with like and stimulating the patient's immune system to fight the problem. Homoeopathic remedies are produced by soaking animal, plant and mineral substances in alcohol; the resultant solutions are progressively agitated and diluted until the dose becomes infinitesimal. The more dilute the dose the greater the effect. Never handle tablets, place them in the cap of the bottle then toss them into your mouth. Patients should not take tablets 15 minutes before or after eating food, cleaning teeth, etc.

Hydrotherapy

Hydrotherapy is water treatment and is used in various forms. The liquid can be hot, warm or cold, steam or ice. It stimulates circulation and aids relaxation, relieves stress and pain. Spas have been popular for many thousands of years and are recorded frequently in many history books. This therapy can be carried out at home using spa equipment which is placed directly in the bath, but these systems are very costly.

Hypnotherapy

Hypnotherapy can also be referred to as hypnosis. Hypnosis is a state of relaxation and a state of heightened awareness induced by suggestion. It has been proved useful for many problems including smoking, alcoholism and drug addiction.

Kinesiology

Kinesiology uses simple muscle testing to analyse imbalances which may occur in the body. A trained therapist may use this method to detect food allergies. The terminology 'Touch of Health' is a name which is sometimes used to describe this treatment.

Massage

Massage is well known to be the oldest form of healing. From childhood most people will recall the saying 'Let's rub it better'. There are many types of massage which involve manipulation by hands on the body's soft tissue. Massage promotes relaxation and healing. For the practising Aromatherapist massage is the most popular method of administering essential oils. It is a skilled technique so do consult a trained therapist.

Meditation

Meditation is usually taught by a teacher in the first instance. Regular time needs to be set aside every day for Meditation which brings a peace of mind and relaxation. Emphasis is placed on breathing awareness and concentration on neutral thoughts.

Naturopathy

Naturopathy is a holistic approach in which therapists believe only nature heals. Diet and exercise are very important and the client is always treated as a whole person. The therapist may use several other Complementary Medicines when treating the client to promote natural healing.

Osteopathy

Osteopathy is widely used today and involves the treatment of the body's bone structure, its joints, muscles and ligaments in the form of massage and manipulation. It can often give long lasting pain relief when the pain originates from misalignment or inappropriate functions of the muscles, skeleton and organs.

Reflexology

Reflexology involves the massaging of reflex points on the feet. There are many reflex points which relate to parts of the body. This treatment can sometimes be referred to as Zone Therapy. A special massage technique can be given which gives relief from pain, stress etc. Self help can be provided at home by using a foot roller which will stimulate and tone the reflexes. Foot rollers can be purchased from any good Health Shop, and battery operated rollers are also available.

Relaxation

Relaxation is a method which can easily be practised in the home to relieve stress and tension. Breathing awareness is very important. There are many classes organised to teach relaxation and many excellent cassette tapes will guide you through the techniques of natural breathing and muscle relaxation.

Shiatsu

The name Shiatsu is derived from the Japanese language. The therapy is a stimulating form of massage using the fingers, thumbs, palms, forearms, elbows knees and feet. Like Acupuncture, Shiatsu uses pressure on the points of the body's meridians. Treatment is carried out on the floor rather than on a couch.

T'ai Chi

T'ai Chi is an ancient Chinese Martial Art. It is a series of graceful movements. T'ai Chi is known to aid the process of healing and improving physical health and relaxation.

Yoga

Yoga is a form of meditation and relaxation which involves physical movements. It is non competitive and participants work within their own ability.

Appendix i

Essential Oils, Associated Products and Workshops

Essential Oils
Essential oils, pre-blended bath oils, pre-blended skin oils, shampoos etc., can be purchased by mail order.

Associated Products
Portable bidets, vaporisers (candle and electric), light bulb rings, foot rollers, body brushes etc., can also be purchased by mail order.

Workshops
Workshops on general Aromatherapy and the use of essential oils during pregnancy and childbirth will be run by the authors. If you wish to take up a more formal training in Aromatherapy write to ISPA, IFA or ITEC for a list of approved training schools. Their addresses are in Appendix ii.

For further information write to:

Eunice & Barbara
PO Box 322
STAFFORD
ST16 2PA

or

Telephone 0785-228866

N.B. The authors regret that they are unable to answer any queries of a personal nature.

Appendix ii

USEFUL ADDRESSES

If you contact any of the Associations/Societies listed below to request information, the Organisations concerned will always appreciate an enclosed stamped addressed envelope.

Action Against Allergy
24-26 High Street, Hampton Hill, Middlesex TW12 (information centre - mail only).

Association for Systematic Kinesiology
39 Browns Road, Surbiton, Surrey KT5 8ST. Tel: 081-399-3215.

Association of Colour Therapists
c/o ICM, 21 Portland Place, London W1 3AS.

Association of Massage Practitioners
101 Bounds Green Road, London N22 4DF.

Association of Qualified Curative Hypnotherapists
10 Balaclava Road, Kings Heath, Birmingham, B14 7SG. Tel: 021-441-1775.

Bach Centre
Mount Vernon, Sotwell, Wallingford, Oxon OX10 0PZ.

British Acupuncture Association and Register
34 Alderney Street, London SW1V 4EU. Tel: 071-834-1012.

British Association for Counselling
1 Regent Place, Rugby, Warwickshire CV21 2PJ. Tel: 0788-578328.

British Chiropractic Association
Premier House, 10 Greycoat Place, London SW1P 1SB. Freephone 0800-212 618.

British College of Acupuncture
8 Hunter Street, London WC1N 1BN. Tel: 071-833-8164.

British Holistic Medical Association
179 Gloucester Place, London NW1 6DX. Tel: 071-262-5299.

British Homoeopathic Association
27A Devonshire Street, London W1N 1RJ. Tel: 071-935-2163.

British Reflexology Association
Monks Orchard, Whitbourne, Worcester WR6 5RB. Tel: 0886-21207.

British Register of Naturopaths
1 Albemarle Road, York YO2 1EN.

British Society of Dowsers
Sycamore Barn, Hastingleigh, Ashford, Kent TN25 5HW.

British Society of Iridologists
40 Stokewood Road, Bournemouth BH3 7NE. Tel: 0202-518078.

British Wheel of Yoga
1 Hamilton Place, Boston Road, Sleaford, Lincs NG34 7ES. Tel: 0529-306851.

Colonic International Association
50A Morrish Road, Streatham, London SW2 4EG.

Council for Acupuncture
179 Gloucester Place, London NW1 6DX. Tel: 071-724-5756.

Council for Complementary Medicine
10 Belgrave Square, London SW1 8PU.

Department of Health
Hannibal House, Elephant and Castle, London SE1 6TE.

Floatation Tank Association (UK)
3A Elms Crescent, London SW4 8QE. Tel: 071-350-1001.

General Council and Register of Consultant Herbalists
Marlborough House, Swanpool, Falmouth, Cornwall TR11 4HW. Tel: 0326-317321.

General Council and Register of Naturopaths
6 Netherhall Gardens, London NW3 5RR. Tel: 071-435-7830

General Council & Register of Osteopaths
56 London Street, Reading. Tel: 0734-576585.

Independent Register of Manipulative Therapists
32 Lodge Drive, Palmers Green, London N13 5JZ. Tel: 081-886-3120.

International Federation of Aromatherapists
Department of Continuing Education, The Royal Masonic Hospital, Ravenscourt Park, London W6 0TN. Tel: 081-846-8066.

Institute for Complementary Medicine
PO Box 194, London, SE16 1QZ.

Institute of Crystal and Gem Therapists
2 Kerswell Cottages, Exminster, Exeter EX6 8AY. Tel: 0392-832005.

International Society of Professional Aromatherapists
Hinckley & District, The Annexe, Mount Road, Hinkley, Leicester LE10 1AG. Tel: 0455-637987

International Therapy Examination Council
James House, Oakelbrook Mill, Newent, Gloucestershire, GL10 1HD. Tel: 0531-821875

MP
House of Commons, Westminster, London SW1A 0AA.

National Institute of Medical Herbalists Ltd
9 Palace Gate, Exeter, Devon EX1 1JA.

National Federation of Spiritual Healers
Old Manor Farm Studio, Church Street, Sunbury-on-Thames, Middlesex TW16 6RG. Tel: 0932-783164.

Professional Association of Alexander Teachers
14 Kingsland, Jesmond, Newcastle-upon-Tyne NE2 3AL. Tel: 091-281-8032

Register of Chinese Massage Therapy
12 Norfolk Road, Cliftonville, Margate, Kent CT9 2HY.

Register of Qualified Aromatherapists
52 Barrack Lane, Aldwick, Bognor Regis, West Sussex PO21 4DD. Tel: 0243-262035.

Shiatsu Society
14 Oakdene Road, Redhill, Surrey RH1 6BT. Tel: 0737-767896.

Society of Auricular Acupuncturists
Nurstead Lodge, Nurstead Meopham, Kent DA13 9AD. Tel: 0474-813770.

Society of Homoeopaths
2 Artizan Road, Northampton NN1 4HU. Tel: 0604-21400.

Traditional Acupuncture Society
1 The Ridgeway, Stratford-upon-Avon, Warwickshire CV37 9JL. Tel: 0789-298798.

Appendix iii

FURTHER READING

Cochrane, A. 'The Fragrant Art of Feeling Wonderful' Mail on Sunday Magazine Supplement, 28-31, November 3rd 1991.

Bremness, L. 'World of Herbs' Chapter 5. 145-169. Ebury Press London. 1990.

Chidell, Lisa. 'Aromatherapy - A definitive guide to essential oils'. Hodder & Stoughton Limited. 1992.

Davis, P. 'Aromatherapy - An A-Z'. C.W.Daniel & Co Ltd, Saffron Walden. 1988.

Hopkins, Cathy. 'The Joy of Aromatherapy'. Angus & Robertson (UK). 1991.

Lawless, Julia. 'The Encyclopedia of Essential Oils'. Element Books Ltd. 1992.

Martin, Gill. 'Aromatherapy'. MacDonald & Co (Publishers) Ltd. 1989.

Price, Shirley. 'Practical Aromatherapy'. Thorsons. 1983.

Price, Shirley. 'Aromatherapy for Common Ailments'. Gaia Books Limited. 1991.

Reader's Digest. 'Alternative Medicine'. The Reader's Digest Association Limited. 1991.

Tisserand, M. 'Aromatherapy for Women'. Thorsons Publishing Group, Wellingborough, Northants. 1985.

Tisserand, R. 'The Essential Oil Safety Data Manual'. The Tisserand Institute of Aromatherapy, Hove. 1988.

Tisserand, R. 'Aromatherapy for Everyone'. Penguin Books, Middlesex. 1988.

Watt, Martin. 'Plant Aromatics Reference Manual'. PO Box 93, Witham, Essex CM8 3DS. 1992.

Westwood, Christine. 'Aromatherapy - A guide for home use'. Amberwood Publishing Ltd. 1991.

Wildwood, Christine. 'Aromatherapy - massage with essential oils' Element Books Ltd. 1991.

Wise, R. 'Flower Power' (Aromatherapy). Nursing Times Vol 85, No 22, 45-47, May 31st 1989.

Worwood, V. 'The Fragrant Pharmacy' A complete guide to aromatherapy and essential oils. MacMillan London. 1990.

Valnet, J. 'The Practice of Aromatherapy' C.W.Daniel & Co, Saffron Walden. 1986.

Thank You

We would like to take this opportunity to record our thanks and appreciation to the following who have supported our publications:-

Alan Povey Signs - 0785-213600 for sign writing and signs.
Aldus UK Ltd and Principal Distribution - 081-813-5656 for the Pagemaker software which has been used in the layout of this book.
British Telecom - 071-380-2316 for providing a fax/answerphone.
Business Initiative - 0782-279013 for financial assistance, business advice and training.
Call Connections Ltd - 0800-238238 for a mobile phone, information and air time.
Jewels & Wainwrights Solicitors - 0785-44116 for their legal help and advice.
Lorraine Electronics - 081 558 4226 for surveillance and communication equipment.
Media Ware - 061-343-3000 for providing help towards the computer system.
Mid Staffordshire General Hospital NHS Trust - 0785-57731 for office accommodation.
Mitac Europe - 0952-207200 for providing a laptop computer system.
MiTeK Computers - 0260-298694 for providing help with the computer system.
Oki Systems (UK) Ltd - 0753-819819 for providing an LED Page Printer.
Panda Press, Stone Ltd - 0785-815110 for help with the printing.
Peter Rogers (Photographic) Ltd - 0785-223810 for photographic assistance.
Quality Analysis Limited - 0376-511773 for analysing essential oils.
Sherry Co - 071 823 4081 for Aroma Diffusers.
Staffordshire Development Association - 0785-277370 for training and business advice.
Staffordshire Training & Enterprise Council - 0782-202733 for financial assistance and business advice.
The Foundation NHS Trust - 0785-57888 for office accommodation.
WordPerfect UK - 0932-580500 for software.

THANK YOU
'Thanks' is such a little word,
It hardly takes a minute,
But there's a world of meaning
And appreciation in it.